More praise for *Report from a Parisian Paradise*

"This book collects [Joseph Roth's] lyrical, often rhapsodizing, journalistic sketches of France. . . . Taken together, these pieces mix nostalgia for a civilized, tolerant, and (Roth knew) doomed Europe with contempt for the Germans—a people, he wrote (prophetically, long before the orchestras at Auschwitz), who 'have always had the gift of killing to music.' "
—Benjamin Schwarz, *The Atlantic Monthly*

"His counterposing of this social flux against his characters' interior motion creates the gentle, biting, clement irony that is peculiarly Roth's own. . . . The specialness of the irony lies in its sincerity. Nothing is being exposed, unmasked or undercut."
—Lee Siegel, *Los Angeles Times Book Review*

"The latest book to join the swelling Roth canon is *Report from a Parisian Paradise: Essays from France, 1925–1939*, which has been beautifully translated by Michael Hofmann. . . . [I]t tracks both the darkening of Europe and the darkening of Roth's own soul. . . . Roth's skill is to take the reader back to his time."
—Alan Riding, *New York Times*

"For his tragic evenhandedness, Roth has been compared to Tolstoy. For his dark comedy, he might also be compared to his contemporary Franz Kafka. . . . In the past fifteen years, Hofmann has translated, beautifully, nine books by Roth. Furthermore, his brief introductions to those volumes are the best available commentary on the writer . . . his prose now mounted to an altogether new level: stately but concrete, expansive but unwasteful."
—Joan Acocella, *The New Yorker*

"Many of the works in this wonderful collection read like the most artful, insightful travel writing and character sketches. Roth is a brilliant observer of cities, big and small—the people who inhabit them and the buildings that surround them. . . . Roth's metaphors are graceful yet telling. . . . This collection, with its timeless and timely themes of war, exile, and identity, should serve as an excellent introduction to a new generation."

—Regan McMahon, *San Francisco Chronicle*

"*Report from a Parisian Paradise: Essays from France, 1925–1939* (superbly translated from the German by Michael Hofmann) offers up a very different yet equally affecting vision of European society. . . . [Roth's] meandering path south through [France] . . . led him to the more familiar, darker places in his soul, a paradox ensuring that Roth's journalistic writing never loses its extraordinary psychological depth." —Laura Ciolkowski, *New York Times*

"The pleasures awaiting a reader of *Report from a Parisian Paradise* are many. Chief among them is the opportunity to get to know Roth better. . . . Here Roth is gentle, sometimes joyful, often sad, but always an acute and imaginative observer. . . . Another of this book's delights is its beautifully crafted prose. Metaphor and anthropomorphism are Roth's natural tools, and he wields them with the deft hand of a master." —Jill Laurie Goodman, *Forward*

"Roth explores with sensitivity and insight the French character, countryside, and culture. . . . Roth's writing has the quality of a camera slowly panning a scene." —*Library Journal*

"One of the greatest newspaper correspondents during the golden age of German journalism brilliantly illuminates the inexorable, deepening chaos that prefaced WWII. . . . Driven to do more than just report, Roth (1894–1939) aspired to define his time, including its calamitous echoes of the First World War. . . . His prose is fluid, often languidly evocative, but then he will suddenly snap lulled readers to attention with bolts of original logic and clarity. . . . [A] haunting and powerful evocation of a world Hitler despised."

—*Kirkus Reviews*

"Joseph Roth was a master of the *feuilleton*, the genre that, always in highly individual fashion, comprises some mix of travelogue, reportage, short story and cultural and political commentary. . . . It is his acute sense for sights, sounds and smells, his insightful intelligence and, most of all, his sparkling prose, captured so well by Michael Hofmann's English, that are important. . . . It is a joy to read, even when the events turn grim." —*Publishers Weekly*

"A laconic but trenchant stylist, Roth remains worth reading for the singular way he imparts the ambience of Europe between wars." —Gilbert Taylor, *Booklist*

"This collection of essays presents magnificent portraits of [Roth's] beloved adopted country just before the world turned dark."

—Steven Robert Allen, *Alibi*

"Exuberance mixes appealingly with bemusement as [Roth] tries to work out what has happened to him, and why he feels this way. . . . His writing achieves simplicity and grace. . . . Michael Hofmann, the translator of this and other works by Roth, has produced a text that reads so transparently and fluently that I felt myself face-to-face with Roth throughout."

—Ralph Amelan, *Jerusalem Post*

"Like other foreigners before and since, [Roth] idealized France, and, as an excursion into nostalgia, his pieces are irresistible."

—Stanley Karnow, *Wilson Quarterly*

"Most astonishing of all, however, is Hofmann's rendition of Roth: his sentences have the ease of simple perfection. . . . It would be a real mistake to expect good news from Joseph Roth, yet there is very good news here, and Roth believed it and reported it with all his heart."

—*Bomb*

Report from a Parisian Paradise

Essays from France

1925–1939

JOSEPH ROTH

Translated with an introduction by

Michael Hofmann

based on an original German selection by Katharina Ochse

W. W. NORTON & COMPANY

NEW YORK LONDON

Manufacturing by The Maple-Vail Book Manufacturing Group
Book design by Chris Welch
Production manager: Anna Oler

Library of Congress Cataloging-in-Publication Data
Roth, Joseph, 1894–1939.
    [Im Bistro nach Mitternacht. English]
    Report from a Parisian paradise : essays from France, 1925–1939 / Joseph Roth ; trans-
lated with an introduction by Michael Hofmann ; based on an original German selection
by Katharina Ochse.
        p. cm.
Includes bibliographical references and index.
    ISBN 0-393-05145-5
    1. Paris (France)—Social life and customs—20th century. 2. Paris (France)—Social con-
ditions—20th century. 3. France—Social life and customs—20th century. 4. France—
Social conditions—20th century. I. Hofmann, Michael, 1957 Aug. 25– II. Ochse,
Katharina III. Title.
    DC715.R787 2003
    944'.3610815—dc22

2003018023

ISBN 0-393-32716-7 pbk.

W. W. Norton & Company, Inc., 500 Fifth Avenue, New York, N.Y. 10110
www.wwnorton.com

W. W. Norton & Company Ltd., Castle House, 75/76 Wells Street, London W1T 3QT

1 2 3 4 5 6 7 8 9 0

Contents

Part III The White Cities

Part IV The Wandering Jews

Part V Parisian Paradise

Part VI In the Bistro After Midnight

Introduction

Report from a Parisian Paradise is, to use Roth's word, a "panoptical" survey of his writing on France, and, as such, a vital complement to *What I Saw: Reports from Berlin, 1920–1933* (Norton/Granta, 2002). Where Berlin represents power, rigidity, scale, and threat, France is suppleness, beauty, humanity, and promise. If Berlin, where the young Roth came in 1920, to exercise his profession and make his name, was a sort of metallic center—"Who in all the world goes to Berlin voluntarily?" he asks in *The Wandering Jews*—then Paris, which he first set eyes on in 1925, was an assertion of independence and preference. The movement to Berlin was centripetal, and informed by ambition and necessity; that to Paris was centrifugal, and an expression of a feeling of professional security and personal blossoming. If Berlin was Joseph Roth's frigid inferno, Paris was his paradise.

It is a rare and extraordinary thing in a writer—especially in a writer like Roth, whom his biographer, David Bronsen, describes as "a seeker, but only rarely a finder," and whom readers would tend to associate with feelings of loss and nostalgia—to find recorded the moment of gain, of joy, of an exhilarated sense that he has come home. (It may, in a technical sense, be "away," but in point of rap-

ture and uniqueness and insight, of a sense of wellness and identification, it can only be "home." In fact, the only other, comparably
vivid instance that occurs to me of a writer finding "the good place"
or "the right place" is that point in the life of the American poet
Elizabeth Bishop when in 1951 she reaches Brazil, marked on page
226 of her volume of letters, *One Art*.)* The laws, the conditions,
under which one has thus far lived are quite suddenly and apparently
irrevocably overturned. It is nothing less than a complete change
of atmosphere, outlook, and expectation, as though the pressure
of three elephants has suddenly been lifted. There is a sudden opening, as though a narrow-angled, specialized, almost defensive vision
suddenly opens to 360 degrees. It is the miracle recounted in "Fos-
terling," in Seamus Heaney's 1991 volume of poems, *Seeing Things*:

> *Heaviness of being. And poetry*
> *Sluggish in the doldrums of what happens.*
> *Me waiting until I was nearly fifty*
> *To credit marvels. Like the tree-clock of tin cans*
> *The tinkers made. So long for air to brighten,*
> *Time to be dazzled and the heart to lighten.*

A SIMILAR MIRACLE befell Joseph Roth when he was just thirty,
in May 1925. He lost no time in communicating it to his friend
and *Frankfurter Zeitung* editor, Benno Reifenberg, in a rapturous
letter dated Paris, May 16:

> Dear Mr. Reifenberg,
>   I hope this letter doesn't give you the impression that I've quite

---

*Elizabeth Bishop, *One Art* (Farrar, Straus & Giroux, 1991).

lost my mind with delirium over Paris and France. I assure you I'm writing in complete command of my skeptical intelligence, and that I'm deliberately courting the risk of sounding moronic, which is about the worst thing that could happen to me. I feel compelled to inform you "in person" that Paris is the capital of the world and that you must come here. No one who hasn't been here can claim to be more than half human or any sort of European. It is free, open, intellectual in the best sense, and ironic in its magnificent pathos. Every cab driver here is wittier than any one of our authors. We really are a miserable lot. Here everyone smiles at me; I love all the women, even the oldest of them, to the point of contemplating matrimony; I could weep when I walk over the Seine bridges; for the first time in my life I am shaken by the aspect of buildings and streets; I feel at ease with everyone, even though we continually misunderstand each other when we talk about practical things, just because we understand each other so perfectly on every subtlety and nuance. If I were a French writer, I wouldn't bother to write or publish anything but just read things aloud. The cattlemen with whom I eat breakfast are more aristocratic and refined than our cabinet ministers, patriotism is justified *here*, nationalism is a demonstration of a *European* conscience, every affiche is a poem, court announcements are as elegant as our best prose, cinema billboards display more imagination and psychological insight than do our contemporary novels, the soldiers are like whimsical children, the policemen witty editorial writers.

This tone of lucid excitement, of articulate ecstasy, is not to be heard anywhere else in Roth. If it hadn't existed in what he wrote about France in 1925 and 1926, you would never have guessed that it was anywhere in his range (or perhaps, for that matter, in any other writer's). The way he is forced to insist on his own sanity to

Reifenberg is a moving confirmation of how strange it is, even to himself! It's a secret further dimension, a wholly unimaginable color. This is the same Roth, incidentally, who, five years later was told, not unkindly, by a successor of Reifenberg's at the newspaper: "Roth, you must become much sadder. The sadder you are, the better you write." This may also have been true, but it wouldn't do to disregard the illumination, the revelation of France to him, particularly in his first series of reportages for the *Frankfurter Zeitung*, called *In The French Midi* (from September to November 1925), and then in the projected short book—sadly never published in his lifetime—to be called "The White Cities." The latter in particular ranks among Roth's finest achievements: the different towns and cities strike the sensitive and adventurous wanderer more like different worlds. The aptest comparison is with the series of exotic planets in Saint-Exupéry's *Le Petit Prince*. These pieces stand in relation to "travel writing" in much the same way as an astronaut does to tourism.

The miracle is there from the very beginning, in the beautiful, limpid opening paragraph of *In the French Midi*, which describes nothing less than a birth into a phenomenologically new and physically distinct world:

> It takes eight hours to get from Paris to Lyons. On the way there is a very sudden change in the landscape. You come out of a tunnel into an abruptly southerly scene. Precipitous slopes, split rocks revealing their inner geology, a deeper green, soft, pale blue smoke of a stronger, decidedly cerulean hue. A couple of clouds stand idly and massively on the horizon, as if they weren't haze but dark stone. All things have sharper edges; the air is still; its waves don't flatter the fixed forms. Each has its unalterable contours. Nothing hovers and havers between here and there. There is perfect conviction in everything, as if the objects were better

informed about themselves and the position they took up in the world. Here you don't wonder. You don't have a hunch. You know.

In its distinctness and otherness this new world poses continual challenges to Roth. Picking his way through responses, distinctions, arguments, he is engaged in continual reevaluation and reassessment. Almost everything, it sometimes seems, needs to be turned on its head.

Here, for instance, is a state founded on a revolution—how enviable/exotic to the poor Germans, with their botched-up, semireactionary, and entirely unloved Weimar Republic! Here—in Lyons—are happy and attractive workers, a twentieth-century proletariat in whom Roth cannot but see descendants of the Roman legionnaires. Here—in Nîmes—is the "cinema in the arena," a contradiction two millennia wide and with all the stars of childhood overhead. Here is eerie, torpid Vienne, with its sleeping dogs and its "silence of deceased stones"; tortuous Tournon with its virtuoso lycée; here is Nice, just along the coast from Monte Carlo, apparently peopled by the slick, deficient imaginations of society novelists; and humdrum Tarascon, trying to do justice to its favorite son, Tartarin, the quixotic bourgeois antihero of Alphonse Daudet. Here are the rivers and buildings and works of art, the swift thumbnail sketches: the boatman, the bootblack, the Sunday bullfighters. Here are the chemical and ethnographic inventories of Marseilles in a couple of lengthy, wonderful Whitmanades; a crowd of smells; a procession of sounds; a layering of sights. Here are the women of Arles, as austerely beautiful as landscapes, and there the erotic landscape outside Avignon, "the smile of the plumped plain between gentle rises," and there is the whitest of the white cities, Avignon itself, a city so beautiful that it calls out to be seduced rather than merely conquered.

Here, apparently turned out of Roth's pockets or plucked from thin air, are exquisite imaginings, phrases to kill for, and distinctions of scholastic nicety: the prison warden, all alone in the Burgundian castle, wandering through the corridors, and making sure he doesn't escape; the rooms in the street of love, where, beside the phonograph and the bead curtains, the children of prostitutes first open their eyes on "the dark of the world." Or the talent parade: "From England arrive singers who can't sing, from America dancers who can't dance, and from all parts of the world naked beauties that are neither naked nor beautiful." And everywhere the physical is turning into the metaphysical, and vice versa. In Marseilles: "What is foreign? The foreign is at hand. What is at hand? The next wave will wash it away. What is now? It's already over. What is dead? It comes bobbing up again." The early writing on France—especially *The White Cities*—is miraculous revelatory prose. Each place is its own conundrum, and its own astonishing solution.

WITH ALL THEIR vividness and externality, these two sequences are also interior. Roth is reflecting conditions in Germany, and also his own autobiography. If *In the French Midi* begins with a birth, *The White Cities* offers something like a psychological *vita*, or a founding myth. Roth gives a dazzling—and not always truthful—account of the experiences and pressures that turned him toward factuality and disillusionment. (A couple of years later he will espouse Neue Sachlichkeit, New Objectivity.) He talks hauntingly—see also "The Children of Exile" (page 00), about what it is not to have had a childhood: "We were the unhappy grandsons who set their grandfathers on their laps, to tell them stories." He writes—as he does in many of his early novels—about his own marked generation, which reached maturity at the time of World War I, and for whom being part of an invading army offered the first experience of foreign travel. His early months in France were a release into happiness, into connectivity, if the word exists. The white cities were what he had once dreamed, and seeing them now gives him back his childhood, completes him as a man. France to him was like the sound of the forge in the twisted town of Tournon; it gave him his bearings, it woke him out of his medieval dread, restored him "to life and human fellowship." Roth in these pages describes the—for him—rare and quite unlooked-for experience of not being *fremd* (a stranger) in a place. It is a state that Lieutenant Trotta, in *The Radetzky March*, needs drink in order to achieve in the frontier garrison town of B.: "Once he'd had a drink, Lieutenant Trotta saw in all his comrades, superiors, and juniors good old friends. He felt so much at home in the little town, it was as though he'd been born and grown up there."

What in fiction—and, later on, in Roth's life—was done by the leveling, calming, beneficent agency of alcohol (though see also "Report from a Parisian Paradise") was earlier performed by what I would call the twin agencies of religion and light. Roth's France lies under the beams of one Apollonian sun and one Roman Catholic faith. At the end of his sumptuous piece on Avignon, he is delighted to quote "the great poet Mistral"* exclaiming: "Races? But there is only one sun!" The sun, too, is "catholic," in the original Greek sense of "general" or "universal," and religion is as general and unschismatic as the sun. The "Fenêtre de l'Indulgence," the first thing to which Roth draws our attention in the Papal Palace is described in a numinous, complex, and half-pagan or -Eastern

---

*Frederic Mistral (1830–1914) was a Provencal poet and writer who led the revival of Provencal literature in France. He was awarded the Nobel Prize in 1904.

iconography: "a wheel with living spokes, curved crosses of light and glass; a round resting place for the light of day; the sun trapped in an artful net." In the same piece Roth praises the "joyful Catholicism that was tolerant of a cult of Dionysus without losing any of its faith and prestige," and offers us the picture of kindly popes watching the people dance on the narrow bridge.

Roth's religion was always an enigma—he was said to have had two funerals, one Jewish, one Catholic—and if his contemporaries weren't certain of it, it must be at least as baffling to us now. Still, I have a sense that, in a cultural if not in a doctrinal way, he equated Catholicism with Judaism, so that Catholicism is either the local variant or else the permissive, universal vehicle for Judaism. At the end of his excitable Parisian letter to Reifenberg he says: "Paris is Catholicism at its worldliest, while remaining a European expression of universal Jewishness." At times "Catholic" almost seems to me his personal code for "Jewish," just as his "Phoenicians"—heroic traders, people of deep culture, "noisy, enterprising, quick-thinking ready reckoners and cosmopolitans," with "open and questing minds"—also come from the Jewish lexicon. And certainly what later provokes Roth's ire, in *The Wandering Jews*, in "The Latin Renaissance," and in his attack on Catholic anti-Semitism in the piece on Bernanos, "The Frenchman on Wotan's Oak," is the failure of Catholicism to remain universal, its reversion or perversion to schism and racism (no better than Germany), and the collapse thereby of his deeply desired, eccentric personal equation: Catholicism ≃ Judaism.

Roth was a walking paradox. In a celebrated passage from another letter to Reifenberg, this time from Odessa, on October 1, 1926, he wrote: "I yearn for Paris, I have not given it up, ever, I am a Frenchman from the East, a humanist, a rationalist with religion, a Catholic with a Jewish intellect, an actual revolutionary."

In order to appear possible to himself, to contain his own contradictions, to assure himself of the freedom of two worlds, Roth sought to couple together such vast, mutually opposed blocks of ideology. As long as his eloquence—and his capacity for self-deception—held, it seemed to work. Overarching constructions and emblems shine throughout his work, and especially in this book with its will-to-optimism: the sun, Rome, Europe, Catholicism, the Mediterranean, a Jewish diaspora, the Dual Monarchy of Austria-Hungary. When they split or realign themselves, the politics, the nationalities, the religions—like the same-pole repulsion of pairs of magnets—his identity and felicity unravel. The blocks, the concepts, the allegiances, the tribal nationalisms he opposed all his life turned on him, and ground him up between them.

To many Germans of the "stab-in-the-back" persuasion, even to visit France would have appeared traitorous. Roth's mission to educate, to soften, to civilize, couldn't succeed with such a barbarously certain cast of mind. Even in 1925, as he first went "across the fence," things behind him were already hardening: the rapidly ossifying World War I general Hindenburg had just been elected president of Germany. In 1926, in what seems to me the pivotal disappointment of Roth's career, the *Frankfurter Zeitung* decided not to make him its Paris correspondent. (Instead, symptomatically, the job went to the Nationalist Friedrich Sieburg.) A casualized and demoralized Roth kept Paris as his base—to leave it, once having discovered it, would have been unendurable—but the joy and hope it had once brought him were largely gone. What he loved about it became more fugitive ("Report from a Parisian Paradise," "The Child in Paris"), and there was more to criticize, and to worry about. In the first novel he completed in Paris, *Flight Without End*, published in 1927, he leaves his hero, Franz Tunda, standing in the middle of the city and in the prime of life, feeling entirely redundant. Roth similarly lost his rapturous feeling of having arrived, and became once more—what he was almost all his life—a transient.

THE WRITING — ONE almost has to say, "of course"—was as brilliant as ever, in the "Parisian Paradise," in the tour of the World War I battlefields, in "The Panopticum on Sunday," but one reads it with a feeling of what it must have cost Roth. He is no longer dissolved in what he writes about, rather he clutches at it or sifts it or plays with it. Following Hitler's assumption of power in Germany in 1933, Roth broke off all ties with the country including those with the *Frankfurter Zeitung*. His publishers from thenceforth were little emigre houses in Holland, and he wrote for precarious German-language outfits in Paris and elsewhere. His world shrank even as it spread. He referred to himself as a citizen of the "Tournon Republic," the few streets around his beloved Hôtel Foyot just off the Luxembourg Gardens ("In the Bistro after Midnight" gives a beautiful sense of what his life and contacts must have been like), and he clung on. For a time he fought back, in "The Myth of the German Soul" or "The Frenchman on Wotan's Oak," but polemics weren't really his métier either. "I play my flute," he wrote, "but the drums are pounding and no one listens to me." The last few pieces here, "Rest While Watching the Demolition" or "Old Cossacks," are almost unbearably moving. They convey a sense of defeat that he did all he could not to acknowledge in his fiction. There is not much in literature—certainly, not much in prose—that one can set beside them.

The last big piece here, "Clemenceau," is Roth's last hurrah. In it he aligns himself squarely and frankly with the "ancestral enemy," and celebrates French patriotism, French suspicion of Germany,

French indomitableness and intransigence. Even here, though, what one remembers are not the pages of Clemenceau's blustering oratory so much as the loneliness of the ancient fighter. Like Roth's last novella, *The Legend of the Holy Drinker*, composed in the same weeks and months of 1938 and 1939, it is about making an ending.

Michael Hofmann
November 2003

Part I

First Impressions

How to Celebrate a Revolution
(1925)

They are dancing in the streets of Paris. People are dancing in celebration of a revolution, a revolution that took place such a long time ago that only a historian can have any faith in the notion that it actually took place. Once again we have the insufferable arrogance of a caste that bears comparison with the one that passed under the guillotine. In spite of that July 14 remains the great popular festival. The annual victory celebrations are so magnificent that people forget that their occasion may have lapsed. The Place de la Bastille is so splendidly illuminated that people remember the great historical illumination; and the crush and swarm of the crowd is such that the great terror of the masses is once again felt—now as then.

They have been dancing for three days. Groups of musicians set up and played in the middle of streets and squares. Grandfathers danced with grandchildren, mothers with daughters, fathers with sons. One of the great cities of the world wanted to be not a great city but a great joy. Public order was replaced by the disorderliness and extraordinariness of the celebration. Chauffeurs left their motors running, got out for a drink and a dance, and drove on. The street, you see, did not belong to them in their capacity as chauffeurs but only became theirs when they danced. The pave-

ment, likewise, was the property not of pedestrians but of dancers.
Who, under these circumstances, would walk or drive?

There was nothing forced in the decorations, nor could the flags
that swung out over crossroads like gaudy bridges of joy truly be
called bunting. They grew out of doorways and flowered from windows. Old walls gave proof of their fertility and sprouted. The celebrations were neither improvised nor contrived. They were an
organic outgrowth of the asphalt, which all year round is such that
musicians might spring from it. Red lanterns hung on the trees but
they didn't look anything like the fruits of the Hesperides. Far from
being pretexts for easy similes, they were nothing but illuminated
red paper, but they looked at home in the foliage. It surrounded them,
and they shone through it. The artificial consorted beautifully with
the natural. And even though the waiters demanded immediate pay-
ment, still it felt as though you were getting everything for nothing—if only because you were getting it in the middle of the
carriageway. The poor man didn't feel he was being extravagant, and
what was bought and paid for still seemed to be free.

On the evening of July 14, there were fireworks. Workers
thronged the streets, while poor rich people languished in big cars
and were hurriedly whisked by. Every gesture straightaway filled
itself with historical content. The lights were not rhetorical.
Advertisements paled in the plenitude of disinterested, joyful light
that shone for the fun of it. Colored, crashing rockets leaped up
from the horizon. Children perched on their fathers' shoulders
and cheered. These children, who will never cease to be republi-
cans, even if one day they become the victims of politics.

Because, at an impressionable age, when a firework is a thing of
grandeur, they have seen the distant flicker of a fire called Revolution!

Essay unpublished in Roth's lifetime

2

America over Paris
(1925)

Over the rooftops of Paris there is a smiling baby colossus of rude health. It is there to promote, to advertise, a soap whose appalling effects it represents in exaggerated form. This huge disembodied baby, whose mouth is fifty feet across, and whose round, vacant eyes perhaps ten, is attached to walls and fences. It's a robust monster—a smile today but a grin tomorrow—a sporty infant with a football for a face, the image of the coming man. It is an idealization of the American male, who has always worn baby shoes so big he never has to take them off: naive and brutal, sentimental and steely, the 100-percent-stroller-pushing champion sprinter. The baby may be the brainchild of a French soap manufacturer, but it's more than just an ad—it's a symbol, a symbol of America: America over Paris.

I can feel the shadow of skyscrapers looming over me, and I have a sense of darkness as I look at the colored, dancing lights offering me shoes, films, fountain pens, and women. The international consumer—who of course is not international but is only called that because he pays in various currencies—in return for his money demands the very latest revues with electric spotlights and hot-air baths and Hoffman Girls* fitted with newest comfort; but also genuine Parisian apaches, and local sensations whose shock effect is guaranteed to wear off. The boulevards and amusement parks willingly adapt themselves to the demands of tourism. Nothing is too cheap for the visitor. Everything is made dear. Sometimes the whole wonderful city prostitutes itself to foreign visitors for an entire season; it remains a wonderful city. The dull hues of neon signs here become living color. And yet, even the forever generative atmosphere of Paris is helpless against the demeaning content and functions that are continually being supplied.

Paris is barely able to digest those foreigners who have come to live off the foreigners who are already here: a great crowd of anonymous and desperate opportunists; swamp-born Myrmidons always ready to amuse, living in "a fever of expectancy." There are the balalaika Russians, who have given up their homeland, and now attempt to refashion it with silk and glitter in the vaudeville, in their nostalgia for the good old days of the czar. Poor people, blinded by the revolution, condemned by fate to make money out of their own homesickness, without any connection to the soil that fed their talents, living only on memories and dated notions that have barely enough substance to drive an operetta. From England arrive singers who can't sing, from America dancers who can't dance, and from all parts of the world naked beauties who are neither naked nor beautiful. Here come tap dancers rattling like skeletons in clogs, and saxophonecians whose instruments creak like the hinges of hell. Here come the tailors who write sketches,

---

*The (Gertrude) Hoffman (1876–1966) girls were a Tiller-type formation group that used a type of athletic acrobatic transformation of the chorus girl, with kicks, leaps, etc.

and the poets who design women's clothing, the lighting artists with their light effects, and the half-Spaniard with his castanets. And only very rarely, among so much suave sophistication and honest amateurishness is there anything like the feminine grace of the Spaniard Raquel Meller, the spiritedness of Mistinguette, the wonderful malice of the wonderful dwarf Little Titch, the beautiful body of a flamenco dancer, and the tragic humor of a Shakespearean clown. These are the real thing, but they are cheated of the effect they should have had in this seething mass of misguided mediocrity—which is somehow worse. People go along to catch them, but also those women who preen back and forth in their ostrich costumes (as if peacocks had borrowed a set of ostrich plumes); to hear the songs barked out by a hoarse set of tails; to watch thirty-six respectably stimulating girlie-legs waving around, turning chaste gymnastics into an erotic exercise. In the intermission (the unremitting intermission), a fat half-breed impresario stages displays of Oriental belly dancing, and has everyday women from Smyrna and Czernowitz perform unwise gyrations on manmade carpets on a nightly basis.

In the narrow lanes of Montmartre, car horns resound with hundredfold echo, harsh imprecations against the venerableness of the walls and the genuineness concealed within them, only to be lured out by a paying public when evening comes. Painted Face hurriedly applies another layer of face paint. The flower-seller's misery becomes quite incredibly miserable. The beggar's handicap is exacerbated. Because *this* auditorium listens to the true singer, the song perforce is false. A world of snobbery spills out of the automobiles. Their painful headlights strip the beautiful darkness from the beautiful buildings. The cars wait in the narrow streets until the visitors have seen enough of the local color for which they have paid a little entrance fee, and then they whiz down the hill, into the modern garages of identikit hotels. It takes many hours for the streets to recover their beauty.

But they do. Not all the many trippers, by birth or bank balance, are able to reduce the beauty of this world to banality, this city with its thousand dramatic spires in an air of glimmer, wind, and evening sky. Millions of restless, nervous chimneys on millions of roofs, a seemingly limitless ocean of dwellings, a commotion diminished to the pluck of a harp, a dramatic exaltation that pulls you down into its depths, like water . . .

Then, all the way up the Eiffel Tower, you see the name of a famous manufacturer, rich enough to afford one of the symbols of the world—and America is over Paris again.

By way of conclusion, here is a letter that reached me today from Paris, as if to confirm everything that has gone before. It reads:

This summer Paris is neither hot nor cold nor rainy; it is American. Everywhere you go, you hear the twang of American English, everywhere you encounter lanky figures in flat shoes, with big horn-rimmed glasses—the women as much as the men—extrawide suits, red Baedeker guides in their hands, and lots of walking sticks and umbrellas. In front of the shopwindows on every one of the *grands boulevards* one hears animated discussion as to whether the items on display are cheap or expensive. Along all the avenues there are tour buses, each crammed with fifty or sixty Americans sitting obediently and with folded hands, almost as if they were at school. A guide stops the coach from time to time, and instructs his flock, which answers him not with a "Baa" but a "Wow!" In all the restaurants the waiters are drilled for American clients; even a Czech, a Russian, or a German, once he orders a meal in halting French, will find himself served by a minimum of five waiters. The bills are likewise made up especially. It is the French I feel sorry for in all this: They are not served at all; they sit there for hours, hungrily and angrily they demand their dinner, which the natty juggling waiters whisk past their noses to the "American" customers. Only in summer do you see so much gold and silver on clothes. The elegant and subtle line of French designers and couturiers in summer becomes lavish and ostentatious: American, in a word. In shoe stores you see curious models without heels, something between a sandal and a sport shoe, made of colored brocade, with gold, with silver, with mother-of-pearl; no Parisienne would be seen dead in anything like that. . . . In the arts and crafts exhibition, one pavilion is taken up by Signora Gallenga's gold- and silver-painted fabrics. Magnificent coats and dresses, decked with Renaissance ornaments. This is where the American ladies like to meet. They spend hours feeling the material and trying everything on. The younger ones, with pert noses and slim, athletic legs, wrap themselves wantonly in those "Borgia" coats, and look like chorus girls. Even the generously proportioned elderly matrons with big horn-rims are unable to withstand the temptation, and they too wrap themselves in a red or purple Renaissance velvet gown—"Wow!" In the Louvre, in front of the Venus de Milo or the Mona Lisa or the slaves of "Michael Angel," they sing out their "Wow!" After dinner, they roost in large concert halls. The cheap seats are all empty, but the boxes and the stalls are bursting. Onstage there are dancers, English-speaking entertainers and acrobats, the inevitable girls in extraordinary getups, because simple nudity is no longer enough. . . . Meanwhile in the auditorium, in spite of the heat, no open necks or bare arms, because all the American ladies are in . . . their furs. Ermine and chinchilla, fox and ermine . . .

Frankfurter Zeitung, August 26, 1925

Part II

In the French Midi

3

Lyons
(1925)

I t takes eight hours to get from Paris to Lyons. On the way there is a very sudden change in the landscape. You come out of a tunnel into an abruptly southerly scene. Precipitous slopes, split rocks revealing their inner geology, a deeper green, soft, pale-blue smoke of a stronger, decidedly cerulean hue. A couple of clouds stand idly and massively on the horizon, as if they weren't haze but dark stone. All things have sharper edges; the air is still; its waves don't flatter the fixed forms. Each has its unalterable contours. Nothing hovers and havers between here and there. There is perfect conviction in everything, as if the objects were better informed about themselves and the position they took up in the world. Here you don't wonder. You don't have a hunch. You know.

In Lyons the thermometer touches 95 degrees. It is very hot. Even so, the streets and people don't feel tired and sluggish, but animated and bright. Everyone talks about "This heat!" thus demonstrating he is well able to bear it. The porter says it, and the driver, and the elevator boy. Only the room-service waiter seems to think it an impermissible intrusion to talk about the temperature. He struggles with himself. At this point I say, "This heat!" and he seems relieved, as though I had somehow cooled him down.

This waiter is as polite as all his other Lyons colleagues. Theirs isn't the submissive politeness of the servant but the proud politeness of hospitality. I am their "guest"—and not in any technical or euphemistic way. Even when they're too busy to attend to me, they still smile. I know they won't forget about me, I know they'll be back. They describe the dishes on the menu without any exaggeration but with elegant persuasiveness. They are a very pleasant change from their Parisian colleagues, who are always calculating and in a hurry.

The people of Lyons are politer than Parisians, and not just because they are calmer and more easygoing, but also because they have more refinement. Lyons is an ancient city; it was founded in 43 B.C. The guidebook says that Augustus built a palace, several monuments, and an eighty-four-kilometer-long aqueduct here. This old settlement is on the right, steep bank of the Saône. Flights of stone steps go up and down between the streets. The buildings go up steeply, their roofs are set like steps. A rack-railway takes you up to the cathedral at the top, which proudly overlooks the city— the old city, the later addition between the Rhône and the Saône, and the new city, which has sprung upon the left bank of the Rhône and is still growing.

They are basically three cities, then, divided by the two rivers, the Saône and the Rhône. Thanks to them, three cities of quite distinct character. It goes to show how much separation water can create. In the oldest part, pre-Christian, early medieval, and contemporary styles come together in a very intimate and living way. Stone, ceramics, fountains, shards, animal carvings everywhere. The stone form of a dog in front of a garden full of roses bears the inscription *Cave canem*, just as they used to teach us at school.

In this oldest part of town, there is no inert historicizing. The old things are on the beaten track. The new life doesn't bloom from the ruins. The ruins bloom into new life. In a museum they might have been cultural bric-a-brac. But here every passerby sees every stone afresh, and everyone has the sensation of being the very first person to see it.

In this city, they weave silk, and export it all over the world. Chinese, Orientals, Spaniards, Tunisians, and Arabs all live together. People work, one would have said, as hard as people work in cities in Germany. But they are also able to take pleasure, to eat and live, in a way in which people can only take pleasure, eat, and live in a French city. A stranger feels less of a stranger here than he does in Paris. No one notices him. Many worlds collide here. Greek, Polish, and Sephardic Jews conduct business here. Silk is a noble product. I think it must be a great pleasure to work with; an even greater one, mind you, to earn money from.

The manufacturers have their villas on the other side of the Rhône. That's also where the workers live—not in villas, alas, but in tenements. I go there for my evenings. It's only among the poor that one can get a sense of what an evening is. For everyone else evening is an extension of their day. For the poor it signifies peace and rest. They sit outside their doors, they wander slowly down to the river and watch the water. The enormous fatigue of the day drops from their hard hands.

Frankfurter Zeitung, September 8, 1925

4

The Cinema in the Arena
(1925)

The arena of Nîmes holds celebrated bullfights some afternoons, but in the evenings it houses a cinema, which is a
rather more cultured thing than a bullfight. Currently, it is playing
The Ten Commandments,* that great American film that has already
been shown in Germany. In the evening I take myself to the arena.

You have to hope it will stay dry, and in Nîmes the chances of
that are good. It rains very rarely here, and never for long. The
stones cool off in the evening. A couple of arc lamps light up half
the arena. The other half is left in shade. The ghostly white forms
of the huge crumbling blocks of stone loom up out of it. They
have already been through so much, these stones. In the Middle
Ages, two hundred families lived in the walls of the arena and built
a church (in one of the spacious arches). In wartime the arena
became a fortress. It survived the changing epochs, and time and
again was emblematic of its era. Now, in 1925, it is no longer a
church but a cinema, admittedly a cinema showing *The Ten Commandments*. At a time when these commandments are not much
obeyed, that's already saying something.

*Cecil B. DeMille's original 1923 version.

In the middle of the arena there's the screen, like a white board in a classroom. In the archway opposite, the projector is purring away. The orchestra sits in front of the screen. The members of the audience (for fifty centimes) are free to wander about on the upper and lower stone seats. Some, who prefer to be cool and lofty, stand on the top edge of the wall, black against the blue sky. It's a most marvelous cinema, cool, clean, without any danger of fire, and much more magnificent than a cinema has any need to be. If any Americans happen by, then surely by next year they'll have put up a big concrete bowl, the largest in the world, with velvet trim, water closets, and glass roof.

Before the show the children play catch behind the screen, and hide-and-seek, and grandmother's footsteps. All the children of Nîmes—and the people here have many children—go to the cinema. The mothers don't forget to bring their infants. The youngest visitors are admitted free, though admittedly they don't see anything but lie on their backs under the night sky, with open mouths as though to swallow the stars.

It seems almost feasible. Hereabouts the night sky is very open-handed with shooting stars. They fall not in an arc, as they do in the North, but sideways, as if the heavens were rotating. There are several kinds of shooting stars. While the sentimental, ocean-diluted Bible is being shown on screen, the best thing to do is watch the shooting stars. Some are large, red, and lumpy. They slowly wipe across the sky, as though they were strolling, and leave a thin, bloody trail. Others again are small, swift, and silver. They fly like bullets. Others glow like little running suns and brighten the horizon considerably for quite some time.

Sometimes it's as though the heavens opened and showed us a glimpse of red-gold lining. Then the split quickly closes, and the majesty is once more hidden for good.

From time to time a large, shooting star falls quite close. Then it's like a silver rain. Each one vanishes in the same direction. Then the apparent quiet is restored to the deep blue, that everlasting fixity of the stars, of which we still manage to feel that they move, even if we didn't know it.

There they are again, the old familiar constellations that remind everyone of childhood, because it was only as a child that one gazed at them so raptly. They are everywhere. There you are, so remote from your childhood, and yet you meet it again. That's how small the world is.

And if you think some of it is foreign, you're mistaken. Everywhere is home. The Great Bear is a little nearer, that's all.

It was a good idea to put on a film in the old Roman arena. In such a cinema you come to comforting conclusions, as long as you look at the sky, rather than the screen.

Frankfurter Zeitung, September 12, 1925

5

Nothing Going On—
In Vienne
(1925)

There is nothing to be said about this town. Nothing happens here any more. Everything has already happened. It's
a town of great uneventfulness. A final peace sleeps in the streets,
from which nothing more will be produced. It's not the blithe hush
of a summer churchyard. It's the forceful silence of opened catacombs: a stone silence that is deader than stone: the silence of
deceased stones.

I spent three days in Vienne, one of the oldest, or perhaps the
oldest town in France. I've stopped waiting for anything to happen. I feel as though nothing could happen anywhere in the world
anymore. It's as cogent as a death to which one has long since
become accustomed: a historic death, a death with sarcophagi
that have long since been sealed: a great departure that is gone
and forgotten.

Vienne has 24,887 inhabitants. Maybe there are a thousand
young people among them. Another two thousand are working-
men and -women, whom you never see. All the rest are children
and old people. By the time the children are old enough to leave
the city, the old people will be on their deathbeds. And then there
won't be anyone left in Vienne. It's a miracle that this hasn't long

since happened! Maybe the ones who were born in Vienne will come back when they feel their death approaching. Because death summons death, the dead call out to the dying—and there is an anticipation of eternal bliss.

It's three days since I heard anyone laugh. I don't see any faces that betray the anxieties of today and tomorrow or the joys of today and tomorrow. I don't see the anguish of the hungry man. I don't see the industry of the busy man. I hear no singing and no music. Only the bells strike in their clock towers, more from old habit than to tell the time. The hands of the clocks turn without regard. This city goes by centuries, not by hours. Its clocks would need to be made like clocks in the afterlife.

I have yet to hear a dog bark here. There are dogs, but they lie in the middle of the narrow streets and sleep. Nothing can wake them. The cats sit on windowsills and in doorways, and are infinitely wise. The doors of all the houses are open. The windows are open. There is no sudden wind that might imperil the glass or the people. And if there were a wind, then neither the things nor the people would be able to sense it. In the evening a few birds set up a nervous twitter. They keep trying. No one hears them. They are discouraged and fly off.

The old women, who are fed and looked after by the cats, are deaf and so blind that they can look straight into the sun, as if it were a feeble lightbulb. And the sun is strong here, it shines with tenfold rays. Washing is hung out to dry on thin lines, not stirred by any breeze. It is a mystery who washed it. I don't think any of those women has the strength to wash shirts. It's my sense that the shirts have been hanging there from time immemorial.

The dwellings in the heavy old walls are like open safes in the vaults of large banks. People lie around in them like items of no value that are not worth locking up. I look through the windows into the rooms. I see a lame man sitting motionless at a table, in front of him a bowl he doesn't touch. His eyes are of green glass, his face is waxen, his yellow beard is a twist of flax. Perhaps he is only hands and head—like the models in the panopticum—and if you detached them, you would see that inside he is all sawdust.

There is a policeman, he is my rival. We two are the only living beings. We know each other, we hear each other's footsteps; they are the only ones that make an echo. But in the evening the constable gets up on a bicycle and glides through the world on rubber tires so as not to disturb the quiet. And then I am ashamed of making such a blasphemous noise all by myself—as though I were clumping on heavy boots through a church full of people praying.

Even so, no one hears me. If I bid one of the old ladies a good evening, she looks at me in amazement. How can her evening be good or bad? It's always evening where she is. At night, little lights are on in all the rooms, only *one* yellow light in each room, not to create light but to draw the shadows out of the furniture.

The old ladies sometimes pray in the cathedral. It was built in the eleventh century. The old ladies sit perfectly still on chairs with woven straw seats, with a continual tremor about their lips, a tremor not of words, but of a strange, soft wind. The church is narrow and elongated, and its ceiling is a dark blue sky with silver stars. On its portals are ten rows of stone crowns. In the crowns live silvery gray pigeons, the quiet Christians among birds.

A couple of streets away is the Roman temple of Augustus, wide and flat, with Corinthian columns. It is open to the wind and the sun and rain and time: It is a heathen temple. Over the ages it has served as a law court, a museum, a library. Today it is surrounded by a fence. You may not visit it anymore, as you might still have visited it in the time of the Burgundian kings, who have their castle opposite and whose children used to play in it. The castle is small, with one tiny tower and narrow extending oriels. I don't understand how, with the example of Roman freedom before your eyes, in the form of Corinthian columns and a temple open on three sides, you can still opt for a small and crooked castle instead. Today this castle is what it always was: a prison. Only, in Vienne there are no criminals, there are not even any drunks. There is just one prison warden, who is his own prisoner. He leads a meaningless existence—like a key that fits no lock or a door without a house. He wanders through the corridors and makes sure he doesn't escape.

Two ancient old ladies live in a courtyard that was once a Roman forum. They never leave their courtyard. They barely notice if anyone enters it. They sit outside their front doors nodding to each other, and sometimes a word passed between them falls down in the courtyard like a small pebble in a deep well: You hear no sound.

Green plants sprout between the stones. They are the same stones that Julius Caesar ordered to be built up into fortifications. They are as dead as Julius Caesar. It's not true to say that stones speak. Stones are silent.

Frankfurter Zeitung, September 15, 1925

6

Tournon

(1925)

In the sixteenth century Tournon was a city of some renown, lived in and visited by scholars and poets. The cardinal of Tournon founded the lycée here in 1542, which was run for a long time by the Jesuits, and where pupils are still taught today. The cardinal had enjoyed one of the most brilliant careers of his time. His monument stands outside the lycée. He looks like a church diplomat—there is an elegant, worldly skepticism about him. He has thin lips and a fine nose, and while his expression, appropriately for a thinker, is one of thoughtfulness, it doesn't quite convince you that it is capable of reaching those far distances that are forever inaccessible to practical intelligence and open only to a wisdom that is not of this world.

For all his fame, the cardinal probably wouldn't have been given a monument if he hadn't founded this lycée, from which many gifted and a few famous Frenchmen have graduated. The memory of the cardinal is kept very much alive in his school. There's probably no better way of ensuring one's immortality than founding a school for young people. Many generations carry the name of the cardinal whose school they attended, if not in their hearts then at least in their heads.

It's July and vacation time; the lycée is closed now and under the care of a concierge, an old and talkative woman, happy to give me her own account of the history of the even older lycée. She is sixty-two, married but childless, her husband is a gardener and very taciturn, grown silent at the side of this woman, who for forty years now has taken the words out of his mouth and saved him the trouble of tedious speech. With what rapture she receives a rare visitor, although her husband is already looking rather alarmed! Thirty years ago she had been in Paris, and even then the noise had been hard to take. Could I take it? I was young and happy? Surely I couldn't be any more than twenty-five, and my parents' pride and joy? And this lycée is so old! She extends the vowel in "old," so much that you feel quite in awe of the walls and feel the weight of "history."

During the summer vacation, when the sun shines steeply down through the school windows and paints silver rectangles in the quiet corridors; when the doors to the classrooms stand open and you see rows of empty desks, no longer and not yet occupied, the desks with the names of their bored occupants etched into them—at this time all schools are so beautiful, they make you want to head straight for the door marked office and have yourself enrolled once more. All schools are beautiful in summer; and a lycée going back to the sixteenth century is the most beautiful of all.

In the park trees rustle above the swimming pool, which is now dry and littered with scraps of paper, bits of string, and tin cans; but the old white corridors are as scrupulously clean as a room that is expecting visitors. Every step you take echoes and reechoes, every sound draws from the walls a low, well-chosen reply, till walking becomes a form of dialogue between foot and stone.

On the walls of the chapel, built by the Jesuits, I read the names of the pupils. They wrote their own names and the names of the girls they loved next to the confessionals, while the confessor, unseen but also unseeing, received rather less specific confessions.

Old Gobelin tapestries of incalculable value hang in the corridors. The most recent of them are from the seventeenth century. They depict biblical scenes, in piety and humility, with a straightforward, childlike simplicity that speaks to children's hearts but also to more guarded souls as well.

"All made by hand," says the old concierge.

Evening comes, the birds chirp, the whole lycée goes very quiet. The old woman goes quiet, too. We walk together in silence like old friends. She has never seen my home, has no knowledge of where it might be, she knows nothing about me, but now both of us know the old lycée, and I know about the life of my companion. There is nothing remarkable about the fact that in the space of an hour I've become this old woman's friend. Here there is nothing remarkable.

Here the only remarkable thing is the town. It is the most uncomfortable location for a town. Tournon is not nestled but rather squashed in between rocky hills. You could imagine that all the little houses had once been running away and had been caught in the deep clefts of this landscape, without any prospect of ever getting out again. The rocks crush the houses, which move closer together, and crush the lanes, which contort themselves in the effort to find a way through, tie themselves in knots, lose their way, climb higher in trepidation, and suddenly tumble down again. The pedestrian can hardly breathe. There is no square, no open place anywhere. There is no market. Unless you were to take the courtyard in front of the castle, which is about the size of a small fishpond, for a marketplace.

The castle presses itself flat against the walls, as though it were afraid to be a castle. It looks permanently locked. Even if it were to open all its doors and windows, there would still be bars in front of them. The castle houses the prison, the police prefecture, and the town hall. It makes it oddly difficult to tell the three institutions apart. The mayor and the head of police sit behind bars just as if they were prisoners. All the inhabitants of Tournon are locked up. They live between skewed walls, in frantic, crooked lanes, under roofs that bow down; all their days are nightmares; the sharp, pointed gables stick into their lives. No one not born in Tournon can find his way around. You get lost here, even if the place has only five thousand inhabitants. But even if you don't get lost, every step you take is uncertain; the houses, while seeming rooted to the spot, are in perpetual motion, frantic with fear, cowed in anticipation; every round arch presses on your shoulders like a yoke as you go through it.

It is exceedingly fortunate that you are only two minutes from the Rhône and safety, two minutes from the great suspension bridge (the first in France), which is light and sways as though its chains were fastened to the heavens, and where you lose the sensation of walking. It's more as though you were yourself holding on to a rope, swinging across to the other bank, a pedestrian and a miracle of technology at one and the same time.

On the opposite side is Tain, flat and small, and without the fearsome confusion of up and down. Tain has a tiny square, with a puppet theater in it. Today they are playing the old story of the shoemaker and the elves, and the cheapest seats are all sold.

The most expensive ones cost one franc, fifty centimes.

Frankfurter Zeitung, September 23, 1925

7

Bullfight on Sunday
(1925)

O n Sunday I travel on to Nîmes. The great amphitheater, which is still in a very good state of repair even though it dates back to the second century, offers bullfights on Sundays. Provençal bullfighters can't hold a candle to their celebrated Spanish counterparts. They have less color, less in the way of ornate costumes, less excitement, and no bloodletting. These bullfights exist, it would appear, under the auspices of the League of Nations. A few young men from the country content themselves with teasing the bull, currycombing it a little with steel combs and tickling it with darts. The bull doesn't die, and the human doesn't perish. Which is not a comfort or an apology. But what else is one to do with such a well-preserved arena? After all, it's good for the state if the people are allowed to blow off a little steam against animals. That's what this expensive arena was built for. The Romans knew that that was preferable to a revolution any day. And the Romans' successors know it too.

That's what I think on my way there, and that's what I continue to think later on, in the restaurant, sitting with the peasants who own the bulls, and whose sons will be fighting them today. The peasants cut their meat from the bone with large, sharpened pocket-

knives, eat delicate little morsels, and drink the good wine of the
popes,* half a bottle of which sets you back as much as an entire
meal, and they have long, wrinkled throats, down which you can
follow the progress of each mouthful, and large, bony, thoughtful
hands. They don't talk much, except for one of their number,
dressed in town clothes, with collar and tie so that he looks only
half peasant, whom they call "*M. le directeur*," and who is the president of the Bullfighting Committee. This afternoon he'll be sitting in a box, and giving out the prizes. Now he's feeling rather
jolly—a short, fat joker, witty and condescending. The dogs of
Nîmes can smell the good bones, and come slinking up to the
table. The kind-hearted peasants lay their bones on a separate plat-
ter—there is, by canine standards, a good deal of meat still on
them—and won't allow the waitress to clear it away. They are good
souls. They take pleasure in the appetite shown by the dogs, and
pat them hard afterward. They sit for a long time over their meal,
order another bottle, and enjoy themselves after their fashion.

Slowly the arena fills up. Grown-ups, children, soldiers, sit
everywhere from the first, lowest row to the highest, and onlookers are sitting and standing even on the rim of the wall at the very
back. The amphitheater is as high as a three-story building. The
stone circles are stuffed with people, who look very tiny in this
round white space. All their heads, in rows and clumps, seem to be
growing out of the stone, like beets on a field. It's as though the
people hadn't sat down but been sown and sprouted. A white
incandescent sunlight lies on the bare circle in the middle. All
around is a fence with many gates, and numerous concealed
entries and exits. Out of one of these gates plunges the first bull,
with a trumpet fanfare, welcomed by the shouts of the spectators

---

*"good wine of the popes"—i.e., The Rhône wine, Chateauneuf-du-Pape.

and dazzled by the painful sun. The bull has come out of a good, cool, dark shed. This arena is like a savage hell to him, of scorching yellow-white light and noise. He lowers his horns and bends his forelegs for a thrust that will save him. But after no more than a second, he can see that there is no way out of this arena. He gallops around the perimeter fence, sweeping away the onlookers, who all vault over the fence nimbly out of his way. As they do so they yell at him, call him names, toss their caps in his way. The bull barges against the fence. But by now the young people are in the middle of the arena. They wave their hands, call out, frighten him. One runs toward the bull, beckons to him; the bull charges him; the man skips out of the way. He is nimbler, he is two-legged, he has associates who will help him by distracting the furious animal, he is incomparably in the better situation, the brave man. He can use all his weapons: cunning, cowardice, two-leggedness, the fence, the exits, the steel comb. The bull has nothing—even his horns have been fitted with little canvas socks to diminish the thrust of them.

The bull is black, strong; the skin bunches round his neck; his good, broad brow has a blueish shimmer in the sun; his eyes are large, perplexed, dark green, and, for all their fury, still tame.

The people who torment him are young, dark-skinned, stupid. Two among them I will always remember: the first one fat and heavy, with a head like a block of wood, a bandage around his left forearm, the fingers crudely carved with blunt tools, the nose short and stumpy, the forehead consisting of a couple of horizontal pleats and a couple of sags, large eyes under tiny lids. For all his weight, he is the deftest of the pursuers. He clears the fence with a high vault. He picks just the right moment to drop to the ground. He spins around five times in a second. He rakes the bull's brow with a sharp steel comb, and the next moment he is gone. He is applauded a score of times, twice honored from the president's box, the music gives him a little fanfare all to himself. Nothing can satisfy his ambition. This is no game. The man hates the bull with all his soul. The animal is his enemy. The man wants the bull to bleed for him.

His associate is swarthy, tall, and thin, with lanky limbs that get in his way. His bony nose protrudes from his face like a knife. This man hates the bull just as much. He uses methods that are even more underhanded. He takes his own clumsiness out on the bull. He unfurls a purple ladies' umbrella and waves it in the animal's face. Pursued by the bull, and shielded by the umbrella, he scrambles over the fence, and then, from his own cowardly safety, he jabs the umbrella into the bull's testicles. Huge laughter in the arena. The audience split their sides. The ugliest appurtenance invented by man becomes a weapon against the most powerful appurtenance of the beast. The fellow couldn't have found a better expression of human dignity if he'd tried.

Bewildered, exhausted, foaming at the muzzle, the bull stops and faces the gate behind which, he knows, is the good, warm, protective shed, redolent of home. Oh, but the gate is shut and may never open again! The people are howling and laughing, and it seems that the bull has learned to distinguish between shouts intended to provoke him, and mere derision. A colossal contempt, bigger than the entire arena, fills the soul of the bull. Now he knows he is being laughed at. Now he no longer has the strength to be furious. Now he understands his helplessness. Now he has ceased to be an animal. Now he is the embodiment of all the martyrs of history. Now he looks like a mocked, beaten Jew from the East, now like a victim of the Spanish Inquisition, now like a gladiator torn to pieces, now like a tortured girl facing a medieval witch trial, and in his eyes there is a glimmer of that luminous pain that burned in the eye of Christ. The bull stands where he is and no longer hopes.

Then up pops my luncheon companion behind the fence—the peasant who was so kind to the dog and fed it—with a long pitch-fork, and digs its two tines into the animal's back to get it going. The bull leaps up, lashes out, scrapes the sand into a cloud, charges the first man who shouts at it, crashes into the fence, gets over the rail, and races along the narrow space between the fence and the spectators. The cheering is gruesome and deafening. Surely it can be heard a mile away.

Oh, and what treats are in store now! We have still to see the proud horseman in red and gold, the sparkling knights, the wavers of red cloths, the throwers of darts. Everything that has happened so far has been an hors d'oeuvre. The kindhearted, well-bred, polite citizens who take part in the game from a safe distance, by calling out fearlessly and brandishing heroic handkerchiefs, the tailors and hairdressers in their Sunday best—they are getting excited. Foam isn't enough for them anymore. They want to see blood, the good fellows!

I won't be there to see the red-and-gold stalwarts. If I had happened to look like an animal among these humans, then perhaps. But a bull would be capable of mistaking my sorry self for a human. My only associate is a little white dog that a woman brought along. The dog barks excitedly whenever someone runs away from the bull. He would like to help the bull. So would I.

But what can two poor pups like us do against five thousand people?!

Frankfurter Zeitung, October 1, 1925

8

Marseilles
(1925)

There are so many masts, I can't see the sea. The smell on the breeze is not salt and air but turpentine. Oil floats on the water. Boats, fishing vessels, rafts, and walkways have been put down in such proximity to one another that you could cross the harbor and not get your feet wet, were it not for the possibility of drowning in vinegar, oil, and soapy water. Is this the boundless gateway to the world's boundless seas? If anything, it's the boundless supply of goods for the European market. Here are barrels, crates, beams, wheels, levers, tubs, ladders, tongs, hammers, sacks, cloths, tents, carts, horses, engines, cars, rubber tubing. Here is the intoxicating cosmopolitan smell you get when you store a thousand hectoliters of turpentine next to a couple of hundred tonnes of herring; when petroleum, pepper, tomatoes, vinegar, sardines, leather, gutta-percha, onions, saltpeter, methylated spirits, sacks, bootsoles, canvas, Bengal tigers, hyenas, goats, Angora cats, oxen, and Turkish carpets get to breathe out their warm scents; and when, on top of that, the sticky, oily, and oppressive smoke of anthracite swathes everything living and everything dead, masks all smells, saturates the pores, fills the air, hovers over the stones, and finally grows so strong that it muffles sounds, as it has long ago dimmed the light. I was looking for the boundless horizon here, the bluest blue of sea and salt and sun. But the water in the harbor is dishwater with vast gray-green fatty eyes. I climb aboard one of the large passenger steamers and hope to catch a whiff of the distant shores the ship has come from. But it smells like Easter did at home: of dust and aired mattresses, of door varnish, of laundry and starch, of burned cooking, of slaughtered pig, of cleaned chicken coop, of sandpaper, of yellow brass polish, of insecticide, of naphthalene, of floor wax, of preserved fruit.

There are at present seven hundred ships in the harbor. It's a city of ships. The sidewalks are made of boats, and the roadways are rafts. The inhabitants of this city go around in blue overalls, with tanned faces, and large, rough, blackish gray hands. They stand on ladders; apply fresh brown varnish to ships' hulls; carry heavy buckets, roll barrels, sort sacks, toss out heavy iron hooks and catch chests; turn cranks, and haul up goods on iron pulleys; polish, plane, clean, and create new disorder. I want to go back to the old harbor, where the romantic sailing ships stand at anchor, and the puttering motorboats, and where people sell fresh, dripping oysters for thirty centimes apiece.

I rent a boat, but we're unable to move. Our oars are jammed together, just like the arms of a passenger on an overcrowded tram. Whichever way we turn, we bump into wood, fishing boats, barrels, chains—those large, jangling, rusty chains that grow in modern seas. We are not in danger. There is no chance of drowning. We could go out without a boat, on this thick layer of oil. But we might be crushed between two wooden walkways that are slowly but implacably moving together to form one large wooden plateau. So we gesticulate, though nobody sees us; we call out, though nobody hears us; we slip away from the chaos of this vast order, and safely reach the perils of the open sea and the wild waves.

Behind me now I have the monotonous song of the water, in front of me the colorful sound of the city, and over my head a great cloud of noise.

I love the noise of Marseilles, first the outriders, the heavy church bells, the hoarse whistles of steamers, the melody of birdsong dripping from blue heights. Then follows the main body—the infantry—of everyday sounds, the shouts of people, the tooting of vehicles, the jingling of harnesses, the echo of footsteps, the tapping of hooves, the barking of dogs. It's a procession of noise.

Gradually the overall white aspect of the city yields gray stripes of streets, the zigzags of hurried, crooked flights of stairs, the forms of people, the colorful flags of washing hung out across the street, the brown tubs outside the front doors, the narrow streaks of grime in the gutters, the gray canopies of the street traders, the dark masses of shellfish, the bright shop signs, the golden windows in which the sun swims, and the velvet green of the trees. I love the beautiful, animated, idle, and pointless commotion on the streets. Most people don't really go about their business, or if they do, the emphasis is on the preposition, the *about*. The exotically clad stranger, having come here from distant shores, wears the costume of his homeland in the thronged streets and feels perfectly at home. He adjusts neither his costume nor his stride nor his gestures. He walks about as on his native soil, his feet feel themselves at home. Nothing can be so exotic as to draw attention to itself. The sidewalks belong to the whole of humanity, the passengers of seven hundred ships from every land.

Here come horsemen from Turkestan, in wide trousers gathered at the ankles, swathing their bandy legs. Then the little Chinese sailors in snow white uniforms, like boys in Sunday suits; the great merchants from Smyrna and Constantinople, so powerful, it's as though they dealt in kingdoms, not carpets; the Greek traders, who never make their deals inside four walls but only ever in the open, perhaps in order to provoke God the more; the little ships' cooks from Indochina, whisking lightfootedly through the evening, swift and silent like nocturnal animals; Greek monks, with long hempen beards; native priests, carrying their own bulk in front of them like someone else's load; dark nuns in the colorful throng, each one an element from a funeral procession; the dusty white confectioners, selling candied nuts, friendly noonday ghosts; the beggars with their bread bags and walking sticks, which are not the props of misery, but scepter and orb; wise Algerian Jews, tall, gaunt, proud, like swaying towers; the itinerant shoe shiners, men and boys, representatives of a flourishing business— and an art.

I think you must have to study for a long time before you are able to pass a soft green cloth over the toe of a boot with maternal gentleness, and draw all the nuances from the leather, from damp-sad matte to the most gleaming, blackest dry. With a faint pop, the brush flies from the right hand to the left. The tin of blacking spins through the air like a ball. Its lid jumps off by itself and skitters to rest in the shoebox.

Meanwhile the customer sits up on a broad wooden throne, and even if there is nothing else regal about him, his shoes soon will be.

Frankfurter Zeitung, October 15, 1925

9

The Boatman

(1925)

The boatman is old. His arms hang down like limp fins from his crooked, asymmetrical shoulders. His eyes are small and have that whitish sheen that old age draws over human eyes. They have seen enough. Gray moss sprouts from his crisp ears. The hands are like two very old faces. The backs of them are yellow-brown, and the thin skin is very taut. But the old fellow's voice is still that of a young man. He talks in very short, simple sentences like those in children's reading primers. Their melody is always a little questioning, the last word drops from a considerable height—and yet it doesn't come to any harm:

"I come from Corsica, sir. Corsica is the garden of France. Napoleon is my compatriot. This is him here. I got that coin in the war. The war of 1870. I was with the navy. I know all these ships, I've worked on many of them. I've been in many countries. I've even been in Russia. And England, Germany, Spain, Syria, Constantinople. I've never been to Paris. You can't go to Paris on a ship. I've only twice in my life been on a train. Second class. That was nice.

"I am seventy-five years old. If I was ten years younger, I wouldn't stay here. I have a pension of five francs per day. You've been my first customer in a week. This boat cost three hundred francs, I sewed the sails myself. I twisted these ropes myself. The oars are sixty francs a pair. And then I christened the boat. I named it after my father. Jacques was his name. You see, there, *Jacques*. In white.

"My father was a sea captain. On the *Sphinx*. That's her over there. We were two boys. My brother was a captain as well. Now he's retired. He gets a big pension. I stay in his house.

"I didn't want to go to sailing school. I couldn't wait to go out and see the world. That's why I'm poor today. My sister-in-law's good to me. We eat supper at eight o'clock. Then I read novels. At the moment I'm reading *The Count of Monte Cristo*. I don't think it's a true story. I think it's made up.

"There you see our cathedral. It's a fine-looking building. I was in there twice. I don't go to church much. All religions come down to the same thing. I'm a Catholic. But I've been in a synagogue. I've been in a mosque. The Muhammadans say Allah. The Jews say Jehovah. We say the Almighty. But it's all one and the same. My friend is a Jew. He was in prison. His wife betrayed him. He almost killed her lover. Now they're both alive. The woman's dead.

"There go the fishermen. They won't be back till noon tomorrow. They carry a lot of nets. A good day for fishing. We have more anglers than trawlers. You should try angling some time. Maybe you'd get lucky. Because you're a foreigner.

"If I had a thousand francs, I could install an engine on my *Jacques*. Then I could go to Corsica. Down there everything's half the price of what it is in Marseilles. This is an expensive city. But I don't pay rent.

"Here's my card. My name's Bouscia Pascal. It's a Corsican name. Our language is close to Italian. We can understand the Spanish as well. All languages come from Latin. Only English comes from German. Latin's the oldest language. Though my friend says Chinese is even older.

"I'll drop you off at the old harbor. You can have a walk there in the evening. Leave your wallet at home. If you have money . . .

"I'm going home now. We're having soused herrings and green beans. Then I'll read. At ten I'll go to sleep. I won't talk to my brother. I've been living with him for five years now. The last time we spoke was two years ago. He had just had his fourth grandchild. His fifth is due in December.

"On Sunday my sister's coming over from Ajaccio. She'll have tobacco for me. But I don't have a pipe.

"Farewell, monsieur. Careful when you get out. Don't jump! And leave your money at home!"

Frankfurter Zeitung, October 17, 1925

10

Nice
(1925)

The town of Nice looks as if it had been dreamed up by society novelists and populated by their heroes. Most of the
characters you see on the promenade and the beach come straight
out of the lending library and the dreams of little country girls.
God can't have created such people. They aren't made of common
clay, but of high-end pulp. Writers spent so long writing about
them that they came to life. Their movements, their walk, their
clothes, their talk, their thoughts, their ambitions, their desires,
their pain, their experiences have all been put through a literary
filter, and all are exquisite and extraordinary. Here, for the first
time, we have the opposite of the usual process: Here are people
who were originally a literary creation, and were then copied out
in flesh and blood. An author dictated a world into a typewriter—
and lo!—it appeared, here it is, it walks and talks, it plays roulette,
dances the Java, and goes sea-bathing.

A whole season in this novelettish world would probably pall.
But three days are restful. You get over the stresses and strains of
normal terrestrial life, of contact with our common worries, and
the jingle-jangle of fighting for our daily bread. In the society of
the sons of Adam, we are caught up in the ordinary whiff of ordi-

nary tragedy. Here in Nice, though, there is the incense of literary tragedy. Here there are only luxury lives. Here are noble creations. Well-paid domestics stood by their golden cradles. Their
whole youth was a *comme il faut* nursery, personally aired by physi-
cians. Their marriage was an extraordinarily shrewd investment.
Even when they die, they won't leave a gap but an inheritance.

For they are not necessary in the usual sense but in the higher
sense. They are there only to prove the novelists right. And they
do it in Nice. In order to get a little excitement into their lives,
they spend a lot of money in Monte Carlo. The rest of us get
Monte Carlo calling on us every day; our whole lives are games of
roulette.

Here, though, the only way someone finds any excitement will
be if he has a lot of money sitting on red or black. All exude serenity. Even the less well off are favored. You can float in the blue
water all day. The sun makes a point of shining without clouds or
interruption, on such good society. The nights remain as warm as
possible, lest the visitors catch a summer cold. The old gentlemen
from England and America take after-dinner constitutionals with
measured tread, every step counted like a drop of medicine.
Meanwhile their sons and daughters dance, make love, suffer, and
marry in accordance with the authors' prescriptions. Old ladies,
ten years younger on facials and diets, go around in short skirts
and eighteen-year-olds' legs, trailing huge gems and adorned by
unbelievably tiny lapdogs, talking about the future, not the past,
like other old ladies elsewhere. Every few minutes, a gentleman
in a topper will glide down to Monte Carlo on the broad, beautiful road, where there doesn't seem to be a speck of dust, a road
that's little more than a corridor for the well off.

Truly nothing bad can happen: The weak will recover their
strength, the invalid their health, the healthy their happiness, the

happy will experience the shot of tragedy they have been dying for, and that will make them happier yet—and if someone shoots himself, then a romantic veil will be cast over the fact of his death, and it will seem somehow admirable. It's a wonderful thing to live among such good society, people who are naked by day and in evening dress at night, tanned and hygienic, clean and well mannered, made of paper and yet of flesh and blood, without the vices that are a consequence of hard work, and so virtuous that the Lord himself feeds them, even though they are not created in his image.

Frankfurter Zeitung, October 26, 1925

11

A Cinema in the Harbor
(1925)

The cinema faces the ships. From out at sea a man who has long lived without the pleasures of terra firma can take out his binoculars and make out the large, colorful posters. The cinema goes by the modest name "Cosmos." Today, it is showing the film called *Red Wolves*.

The Red Wolves are a band of robbers in the Abruzzi. They have kidnapped the beautiful Margot and hidden her in a high tower miles from anywhere. Ah, but what is miles from anywhere, how high is high? A brave young man by the name of Cesare joins the Red Wolves, but only for appearances: What he really wants is to free Margot.

You probably imagine joining a band of robbers is a simple matter? Let me tell you! It's incredibly difficult. You need to take a battery of tests, in wrestling, in knife fighting, and in arm wrestling. This series of tests makes up most of the film. Cesare comes through them and gains the applause not only of the Red Wolves but also of the audience here, who dream of being robbers in the Abruzzi.

The film about the Red Wolves is screened eight times a day, from ten in the morning until midnight. Cesare passes his tests eight times a day, and eight times the audience gets enraptured, a third of them spending the entire day in the cinema.

This one-third are women and children. By day it's cooler in the dark cinema than it is in their own cramped apartments and in the even more cramped streets. So the women go there to cool off. Children get in for nothing. Every adult visitor brings at least four children with her. She pays for one seat and occupies five.

In the evening the men, dockworkers in the harbor, come along. They eat, they wash, and they go to the cinema. They watched and cheered Cesare's deeds yesterday and the day before yesterday. But it's not possible to see enough of such heroism, if you are nothing more than a dockworker—with the dream in your heart of being a robber in the Abruzzi.

Even more romantic than a harbor is a robbers' cave in the Abruzzi. The day laborer who is today a fisherman, tomorrow gets taken on as a seaman, and the day after finds himself in a distant port watching the film about the Red Wolves finds his life insufficiently romantic.

I like to imagine the robbers in the Abruzzi going to the cinema to see a film about the sea dogs of Marseilles. The robbers in the mountains envy the men of the port. The robber treats his calling as a humdrum job, and dreams of something romantic and exotic elsewhere. It is these reciprocal yearnings that make the film industry tick.

And yet the men in the harbor have roughly the same traits as the men of the mountains. The dockers stab with Corsican knives; they are passionate arm wrestlers with their friends, and stage wrestling matches with their colleagues. They are pleased to see that these same recreations are also popular in the Abruzzi. While still sitting in the cinema, they pull out their knives, and, not taking their eyes off the screen, give their neighbor a playful little stab.

The neighbor, who doesn't stand for this sort of nonsense, challenges his friend to step up in front of the screen and make like Cesare.

So in the cinema, you don't just see the deeds of the men of the Abruzzi but also those of the men of Marseilles.

Meanwhile the pianist keeps banging out La Fille du Régiment. No wonder the viewers are getting restive. They want a different tune. The pianist gets up, walks out, and the film continues without music.

A little later I see a large, angry-looking man. He's not putting up with the piano player's rudeness. One knows what it means when a very large, very broad man, with a broad red belt slung around his hips, with about one inch of forehead and with hands like iron shovels, won't stand for the impertinence of a tiny piano player in evening dress and umbrella.

Five minutes later the pianist is wriggling in the iron grip of the irate cinemagoer, the lights go on, and everyone laughs. The giant waves to the crowd with his left hand, plunks the pianist down in front of his instrument, and decrees the tune desired by the majority.

And the film carries on.

I'm sitting between two children, who are playing marbles on my knees. They are two beautiful, dirty children. I should like to stroke them. The children steal each other's marbles and hide them in my jacket pockets. Their father lights a match and holds it to my face. He wants to know if his little ones are safe with me.

"Beautiful children!" I say.

"Just tell me," he says, "if they start squabbling."

I think he likes me. He has seen that I can keep an eye on his children, and he turns to attend to whatever events are now in progress, be they on the screen or in some other part of the cinema.

Frankfurter Zeitung, November 4, 1925

Part III

The White Cities

12

The White Cities

I became a journalist one day out of despair over the complete inability of all other professions to satisfy me. I was not part of the generation that marked the beginning and end of its adolescence by scribbling poems. Nor did I belong to the very newest generation, which reaches sexual maturity by way of soccer, skiing, and boxing. I could never do more than ride a bicycle—I couldn't even freewheel—and my literary talent was confined to making precise entries in a diary.

I've never been sentimental. Ever since I've been able to think, I've thought mercilessly. As a boy I fed flies to spiders. Spiders have remained my favorite creatures. Of all insects they and cockroaches have the most intelligence. They rest at the centers of circles of their own devising, and depend on chance to feed them. All other animals hunt for their prey. But the spider is a sensible, even a wise creature, because it has understood that the desperate hunting and chasing that other species go in for is useless, and that only waiting is profitable.

I always enjoyed reading about spiders, and about prisoners who whiled away the grim solitude of their cells with pet spiders.

They stirred my imagination, which was a thing I had in abundance. I have always dreamed vividly, but with an alert mind. I never mistook my dreams for reality. And yet I can sometimes immerse myself in them so far that they become a second, an alternative reality.

When I reached the age of thirty, I was finally allowed to see the white cities I had dreamed of when I was a boy. I had a gray childhood in gray towns. My youth was a gray-and-red affair of military service, barracks, trenches, and hospitals. I traveled to other countries—but they were enemy countries. Never would I have guessed that I would make my way so briskly and violently through part of the world, under orders to shoot, rather than with the desire to see. Before I had begun to live, the whole world was open to me. But as I began to live, I saw that this open world had been ravaged. It was I who had destroyed it, I and my contemporaries. Children of other generations, those before, those after, are permitted to find a stable relationship between childhood, manhood, and old age. Of course they may encounter occasional surprises. But not so much as to overturn their expectations. Not in a way that mightn't have been predicted. It was only our generation who experienced the earthquake, after having counted on the complete security of the earth from the moment we were born. We all were like someone who gets on a train, with the timetable in his hand, to travel and see the world. But a storm blew our train away, and in no time at all we found ourselves at a point we didn't expect to reach for another ten years—ten years of ease and color and trauma and delight. Before we could experience anything, it was upon us. We were outfitted for life, only for death to greet us. We were still standing in bewilderment at our first funeral procession, and already we were lying in a mass grave. We knew more than the old people, we were the unhappy grandsons who put their grandfathers on their laps to tell them stories.

From that time forth I have never believed in getting on trains, timetable in hand. I don't believe it is in us to travel with the serenity of a tourist, equipped for anything. The timetables are wrong, and the books are misleading. All travel books are dictated by a stupid spirit that can't see that the world is continually changing. But in the space of a single second, everything can be transformed a thousand times over, disfigured, rendered unrecognizable. People talk about the present with an air of historic certainty. They discuss a living foreign people in terms one would use of one that had died out in the Stone Age. I have read travel books about countries in which I have lived (and which I know as well as my homeland, and which, indeed, perhaps *are* my homeland). How much misreporting from so-called good observers. The "good observer" is the sorriest reporter. He meets everything with open but inflexible eyes. He doesn't attend to what's going on in himself. But he should. Then at least, he would be able to report on the voices he hears. What he records is the voice of a single second. But who's to say what other voices might sound as soon as he's left his post? And by the time he's set down his impression, the world has moved on.

Before we can set down a single word, it's changed its meaning. Our familiar concepts no longer match the realities. The realities have grown out of the tight clothes we've put them in. Ever since I've been in hostile countries, I no longer feel foreign in any of them. I never go "abroad" anymore. That's a leftover notion from the days of the stagecoach! At most I might go somewhere "new." And there I see that I had already intuited it. But I can't "report" on it. At the most I can say how the experience felt, *to me*.

———

I WAS CURIOUS to see how things looked on the other side of the fence that surrounds us. Because we are surrounded by a fence, those of us whose job it is to speak to the German world. In Germany there is a cult of the "concept." We believe in labeling. Germany is where they have the "most trustworthy" guides, and the "most thorough" research and investigations. Everything written down is law. People put their trust in a book from 1880. (They shouldn't even believe one from 1925.) People believe, as they did before the war, in the meaning of the old concepts.

Across the fence, on the other side, the names given things— the labeling—was never that important. The names always hung off things, they were loose-fitting garments. There wasn't the continual endeavor always to have things set in stone. Over there, on the other side, people are continually changing. We are apt to call this "unprincipled"; to us adjustment or accommodation is halfway to treason. On the other side of the fence, I recovered myself. I acquired the freedom to mooch around with my hands in my pants pockets, a cloakroom ticket stuck in my hatband, a tattered umbrella dangling from my arm, among ladies and gentlemen, street singers and beggars. On the street and in society I look just the way I do at home. Yes, and I *am* at home there. I know the sweet freedom of not seeming to be anything more than what I am. I don't represent, I don't exaggerate, I don't deny. And even so I don't catch the eye. In Germany it's practically impossible not to catch the eye unless I playact, unless I deny, unless I exaggerate. And I am given the difficult task of choosing how I would like to appear. For, even if I don't represent any type, any genus, any family, any nation, any tribe, any race, I am still forced to be representative of something. We are forced to "show our colors," and not just any color either, but one off the official color chart: To be otherwise would be accounted "unprincipled." It's the mark of a narrow world that it mistrusts the undefined. It's the mark of a wider one that it permits me to be. Neither has it come up with a label for me. But whether it calls me one thing or another, there's always space between the term and what it applies to, because the world isn't so terribly literal. We are, however, because we confuse names and things.

THAT'S WHY we don't understand the world, and why it doesn't understand us. On the other side of the fence it's vacation time. Lovely, long summer vacation. People don't take me literally. What I leave unspoken is heard. My every word is not a confession. Every lie is not wicked and unconscionable. Every silence is not enigmatic. Everyone understands it. It's as though people don't question my punctuality, even though my watch is wrong. People don't make inferences about me from what's mine. No one controls my day. If I waste it, so what, it was mine to waste.

I FOUND the white cities just as they were in my dreams. If you find your childhood dreams, you become a child again.

It was more than I dared hope. Because my childhood is quite irrecoverably remote from me, separated by a global conflagration, a world on fire. My childhood was nothing more than a dream itself. It was expunged from my life; years that hadn't disappeared, but were dead and buried. What happened next was like a summer without a spring. I came to this country with the skepticism that is the consequence of a life lacking a childhood. Everyone of my generation is "skeptical" in that way. And while the older generation keeps urging us to "rebuild" and "be positive," we smile the knowing smile of those who have been the cause, the instruments, and the victims of a massive destruction. Oh, if they hadn't made us so mute, we could tell them a thing or two about "rebuilding"! We have so little belief in it, we wouldn't even be able to explain its impossibility. The father who has lost his son knows less of destruction than his dead son does. Anyone who was behind the lines has only seen the end of the world in a sort of long historical perspective, it was our great war, our equivalent to the Punic Wars of Rome and Carthage. He would learn the war of his own time out of correspondents' reports, just as he learned the wars of the past from history books. It makes a difference whether you learn something from personal experience or vicariously, from the personal experience of your sons.

We are the sons. We have experienced the relative nature of labels, and of things themselves. In the space of a single instant, which was all that came between us and death, we broke with an entire tradition, with language, science, literature, art—with the whole belief in culture. In that instant we knew more about *truth* than all the truth seekers in the world. We are the resurrected dead. We come, laden with all the wisdom of the hereafter, back down to the ignorant earthlings. We have the skepticism of metaphysical wisdom.

Everything that has befallen us, in the North and in the East, since our return to life, has only strengthened our skepticism. We kept moving away from our childhood. It was as though we had returned, only to be put through all that devastation again. And we, who were pulled out of our history classes on the Thirty Years' War and plunged into the World War, we have the feeling that the Thirty Years' War has never stopped in Germany. We are unable to believe that there can be peace anywhere in the world, and that the great and mighty cultural traditions of antique and medieval Europe are alive still. Since our resurrection we have experienced the rise of a wholly new culture, the revolution in the Near East, and the soft tremors of the Far East, and at the same time the technical wizardry of America. Caught in a land where the same people exhibit on the one hand an infantile longing for the recent past, and on the other a desire to transform man from a being of flesh and blood into one of iron and steel; a peculiar land where half the nation is capable of simultaneously admiring such different and contrary phenomena as army parades and toy balloons; where sensibility is as pronounced as technical expertise—we experience hourly the little struggles and the great wars between past and future—we are equally helpless before the classical, Catholic, European influences of the West, the East and its revolutions, and capitalist America. There is a war brewing that will last for more than thirty years.

Because it is war, and we know it, we—the expert witnesses on battlefields—we understood right away that we have come home from a small battlefield to a great one. Each time we leave this country, we feel like we're going on vacation. How peaceable and innocent everything still is down below! How little the world knows of the avalanches that are in store. Will they not come this far? Will their force be already broken? Will the new culture, preceded by waves of destruction, stop in front of the living monuments of the old, as once before, and strike a compromise?

Happy land of my childhood that is sheltered from storms and has time for thought and time for peace conferences, while we are exposed to the first, uncomprehending, and intractable fury of the elements! Happy land in which one can dream again, and learn to trust the energies of the past, which we thought—like so much else—a mistake and a lie in our schoolbooks!

The sun is young and strong, the sky is lofty and deep blue, the trees dark green, ancient, and pensive. And broad white roads that have been drinking in and reflecting the sun for hundreds of years, lead to the white cities with flat roofs, which are as they are to prove that even elevation can be harmless and benign, and that you never, ever fall into the black depths.

13

Lyons

It was on a Sunday afternoon that I arrived in Lyons.

This city lies on the border between northern and southern Europe. It is a city of the center. Equally amenable to northern seriousness and single-mindedness and to the easygoing South, it smiles and works. Its weekdays are hard and its Sundays full of festive commotion. All its inhabitants are busily doing nothing. They celebrate with impressive assiduousness.

They make silk in this city. The business districts are full of it. All the signs refer to silk. In every shopwindow you see silk. All the women wear silk, even poor working-class women.

Are poor people who weave silk ten hours or more each day in any way better off than their fellows who produce merely burlap sacks? They don't earn any more. You can't eat silk. Social science isn't used to computing the value or refinement of the product as a factor in the weal or woe of the workers.

But it's my conviction that it does make a difference whether you produce silk dresses or burlap sacks. A little glimmer of the deluxe product touches those who make it. And just as coal miners are the saddest workers in the world, so I think silk weavers are among the happiest, after confectioners. If someone spends twenty years weaving shiny, luminous, glowing threads in all the colors of the rainbow, then his soul will be cheerful, his hand tender, and his brain apt to think consoling thoughts.

He will live, admittedly, in a tenement on the other side of the Rhône, on a long, wide, bleak street—one of those streets that yesterday was new, cheap, and hygienic, and today is only cheap. It's striking how quickly new proletarian districts age in all cities. The building materials keep improving, healthy green trees are planted along the edge of the pavement, sewers are dug, running water is piped in, drainage pipes are plumbed, china basins and toilets and rustproof fittings installed. A couple of years later the china is cracked and besmeared with sticky yellow grime, the trees look gray and suffocated under their thick layer of dust, the sewers are choked, the water pipes cracked, the ceilings leak, and the only reason the iron fittings aren't rusty is because they've long since disappeared. Walls blacken, the stucco drops off, and the houses stand there looking as if they've got leprosy. This is no dignified old age but a rapid attrition.

Silk factories are just as bleak and bare and crude as every other factory the world over. But the silk workers are cheerful. They lean out of their windows in the evening, like people who are looking forward to a couple of days off, with time on their hands to take an interest in what other people are doing. The girls in the silk factories are slender brown princesses who live in the dark tenements for fun, not because they have to. Little princesses, forever stepping out of the grim doorways. The men like a drink and are seldom drunk. There is no sound of rowdiness or strife from the bars. The women sit in groups on the banks of the Rhône, fishing or reading the newspaper by the dying light. They gaze at the big beautiful river, which was one of the most important highways of the Romans. Roman men and women must have sat like this two thousand years ago—the soldiers and their wives and sweethearts.

I like spending my evenings here. There are little shops with dusty windows, and the sort of plain, simple goods that only poor people buy: tobacco pouches and heavy watch chains and elephants' tusks and little green china dogs and cats and coffee cups with just one crack in them, and wooden napkin rings and glass beads in all colors, and a nickel toothpick dispenser. There are the little delicatessens, with dusty and only slightly squashed or bruised fruit, with onions and potatoes, newspaper for wrapping things, cats sitting on the food, and little children playing outside. Everything is slow and calm. The hours go by more quietly and easily. Even surprises can be seen in advance. Joys are quieter and more inward. Death is accepted like a gift. Life has no inordinately high value. Life is worth about as much as a weekly wage, a bottle of inexpensive wine, and the cinema on Sundays.

It is in this part of Lyons that I feel the closest to its old history, even though there are no monuments here and the buildings are all new. It seems to me that poor people have the most living connection with the past, they are the last to take on the hasty novelties of the present, they are the most devout in their relationship to tradition. They are "the people," and in their features I can discern the physiognomies of the Romans who first arrived in this city some eighteen hundred years ago, and never left. The poor cannot travel, they stay where they are, they have a narrow geographic horizon, they marry girls who grew up in the next street, and while they don't keep a family tree, it's clear to see, even without any written genealogy, for anyone who can read faces, that they go back to "antiquity" and that historic blood runs in their veins. Simple men, sitting and chatting on the riverbanks, while the evening shadows and red shafts of the dying sun sharpen their profiles, and raise them out of the everyday and invest them with near-symbolic significance: In this man or that I can see a Roman centurion, I set a glittering helmet on the poor man's head, with a curved boss of shining brass; I drape a red shirt around his chest, and over it a breastplate of steel scales; and into his stout, peaceful, innocent fist, I press a short, two-edged sword, hollowed out halfway up the blade, and with two curved blades, smooth, tapering, and lapping like a tongue: and there we have him—a Roman.

And I love the washerwomen on the Rhône. They too are poor, and their first and second youths are firmly in the past, but they are as merry as young girls. They stand there from six in the morning till late at night, and they want to make use of the last, feeble sunbeam, and it's as though they were economizing with the precious sun, and could manage to get three days' worth out of one. The water flows past them, always new silver water; they see millions of waves every day, and in each one they dip a piece of washing; with the gestures of priestesses they wash out the dirt, and the profane becomes sacred. They are bright and merry as the water, they sing all day long, and they call out greetings to one another. Their voices ring out on both sides of the river, mingled with the splashing sounds of the water, extended and refined by the echo of the steep banks, silver bridges, invisible, only for the ear to hear—bridges for greetings. The whole city's laundry is cleaned in the Rhône. It's as though all the dirt is washed off the people; as if these women stood here all day to keep the souls of the Lyonnais clean. And I think that a city that's built on two rivers must have a decent population. Water is a holy element.

Tomorrow morning I will walk over the big Wilson Bridge into the middle part of the city, where the silk is sold. This part of the city is best at eleven in the morning. That's when the grand old office buildings stop for lunch, and the office girls come rushing

out as if to meet their happiness. For half an hour all the inhabitants of the city are rushing toward their happiness, and there's a
great bustle in the streets, and a tooting from the vehicles in which
the silk merchants and manufacturers are sitting. The whole city
becomes like one big fair, the restaurants and bars fill up, and
musicians set up in corners and in little old lanes and play fiddle
and mouth-organ and cymbals, and the girls buy the scores from
them*, and go for lunch with the security of the everlasting,
unloseable, printed music. And you hear the honking of car horns,
the clatter of harnesses, and the rattling of the steel shutters coming down in front of the shops, and for an hour people prepare for
the magnificent, lofty festival that in the white cities of the South
of France goes by the name "lunch."

And then the festival is at hand: the lunch break. From the
street, you can hear the clocks ticking inside the houses, the low
voices of people talking, and the silence is big and white and full
of sun, light without shade, a pause full of nobility. I can see the
typewriters at rest in the offices, under their black oilcloth covers,
and the inkwells with their lids snapped shut, and I can envision
the narrow green ledgers lying in desk drawers, the records of
wealth, and the silk threads—the millions of silk threads in the
large weaving machines—awaiting the completion of their transformation into shimmering fabric.

This evening, I want to go to the beautiful "Fourvière." I've
already been gazing up at it for a long time, like some humble,
naive early man looking up at a symbol of a transcendental power.
Because that's the way the cathedral looks up there, its broad face
toward the city, four columns, three gates, a gable above them,

*One such ballad-seller—performing a song, and selling the sheet music—is at
the center of Rene Clair's film, *Sous les Toits de Paris* (see p. 202).

with a cross on it like a flower, flanked by two round towers as if by guards, and down below, the steps, flat, wide, and many of them, not steps you climb up but rather ascend while genuflecting. The Roman forum once stood here, on exactly the same spot. Emblem of a different force, it yielded up its place, and even a few of its stones, toward the construction of a small chapel, it's still the same flesh and blood—the stone equivalent—as the forum. One symbol has transformed itself into another, the same stone served a vanished power with the same loyalty with which it now consecrates itself to a new, and both of them can put their trust in its fixity. Every year devout people from all over Europe make their pilgrimage to these stones.

The original chapel dates back to the ninth century, grew in reputation and name, was richly endowed by Louis XI, by Louis XII, by Louis XIII. But not until the plague threatened to wipe out the city in 1642 did the hill with the chapel demonstrate its miraculous power; people fled up to it and survived, and since that time the processions wander up to the Fourvière every September 8, and the archbishop blesses the city. The new cathedral was built as recently as 1896. It cost fifteen million francs—money raised mainly from the devout poor.

The cathedral was built to be an emblem of the city, and show its face to the world. And I have never seen a monument from modern times whose grandeur is so intimately paired with tenderness, whose bulk stands back so modestly behind the gentle effect of its details. Saints bear the gable, supporting it on their heads, saints line the recesses of the arches, and so alive is the effect of human forms fulfilling technical functions that every stone seems to breathe as part of some living whole, and the entire colossal completed edifice seems still to be in the process of construction. And even though these statues will always prop up these stones, it still looks as though they are only briefly, provisionally, where they are. In a moment they will move, and the church will wander down to the people, already it's on tiptoe, coming to meet the pilgrims on September 8, the sacred day.

The entire hill is sown with stone steps, and every lane is a staircase, and the old houses built of stones cut from the old fortifications, with bright roofs of an iridescent slate that looks like mother-of-pearl, stand ranked, each one a head taller than the one before, on either side of the steps, always closed, always silent, as if they had taken a vow of silence for an entire year, till the arrival of the pilgrims. Then the doors will be thrown open, jugs of water and wine will be carried out to welcome the devout pilgrims, and on every step there will be one being refreshed. Every last doorstep will have its own guest. Today it's only the gaudy goldfinches and yellow canaries that twitter in their idyllic green cages outside the doors, next to the tidy mailboxes, of which each house has four or five, to save the postman the trouble of going up and down the steep stairs inside.

Right behind the cathedral is where Rome—a living Rome—begins. All the things brought to light by excavations have simply been left where they are instead of being carted to a museum. Every visitor feels the delight of being the first discoverer. The Roman vase stands in the living flowerbed as it did eighteen hundred years ago, and the living gardener uses an antique stone watering can, and at the entrance to the garden you see the Roman dog, with the inscription *Cave canem!*, a primitive sandstone dog, part lion, something of a wolf, a bit of a bear, and all the more terrible for its compounded beastliness and yet as innocent and lighthearted as the memory of my Latin grammar classes. I envy the high school pupils of Lyons. Not even grammar is abstract for them. Every rule is hard and fast. Every exception is marked on the side of the path.

Every stone holds a historical disquisition. Here is a road that leads straight to Rome, into antiquity; this is the way they came here; this is where they crossed the Saône; this is the hill they climbed to survey the countryside; beyond the river is where they started piling up the stones and they pitched a fort, as nowadays you pitch a flag.

From this point, I can see the full extent of the first of my white cities. Yes, this is how it was in my dreams. It's all still standing: the shimmering houses; the white walls bathed in sunlight; the flat, iridescent rainbow roofs; the skipping chimney flues puffing out little blue clouds like little building blocks for heaven. Streets of white chalk, winding away into the green fields, hurrying to meet the dark green forests and blue rock formations on the horizon, on the other side of which lies Rome, the heir to Greece and our first schoolmarm. All alive, all still alive. I hear the heavy chime of the bells in medieval church towers, the sounds of the Cathedral of Saint-Jean ride into the flowering stones of antiquity, and here are the sharp, pointy little towerets of Saint-Nizier, the little roofs armed with sharp hunchbacks and spikes and graced at the top by the conciliatory cross.

Shades of evening settle over the world, the voices of the street fade, the rushing of the Rhône grows louder. I can still make out the town hall, the city library, the church of Saint-Martin, with its heavy fortresslike walls. The moon rises behind the rocks, and the white city becomes still whiter, the stones vie in brightness with the moon, and in blissful harmony the Rhône and the Saône flow on, the one torrential, the other thoughtful, toward the long-desired union that is their shared goal, and they clasp the white city in their arms like a costly possession they will never give up.

14

Vienne

In a museum in Lyons I saw a small-scale reconstruction of Vienne as it would have been in Roman times: It lay nestling between hills, gently climbing on one side, level on the other, either side of the Rhône; and with all its loveliness, it still had some of that Roman monumentality, of the aspiration to eternity that Rome gave to all its buildings, monuments, and settlements. The hills bracketed the town without constricting it. There was still room enough to grow and spread out. There was still green in amongst the stone. The town grew out into the country, and the country pressed itself against the town. Nature and art were equals. The hand of man worked with the materials of the earth. The material was nowhere forced. It gladly adapted itself to the will of man. The life of the town was concentrated in twelve principal buildings. And yet it was a large town. It had no streets, only squares, almost no houses, only palaces. And yet this reconstruction showed something of metropolitan allure, of a sort that no contemporary metropolis can offer. I had the feeling that a man in the setting of a colossal arena remains a man; a skyscraper reduces him to an ant. How is it that you don't feel lost on a wide Roman forum the way you do on a modern boulevard? Roman greatness is not gigantic but human. Rome measures with earthly scale. Grandeur and monumentality have a "human" character.

With this image in my head I came to Vienne. How changed it is! It has always, almost from its beginning, been a capital, a seat of kings and princes. It has belonged to several different nations, and it has changed over time, but none of its temporary masters ever dared to reduce it to a second-class city. It was always young, proud, beautiful, and expansive. It could look into the future without fear, like a goddess immune to the depradations of time.

The city of Vienne has died in the fullness of her beauty, and in this way she really does resemble a goddess. She is not used up, not worn out. She suddenly stopped being a large, beautiful, proud, venerated city. She wouldn't agree to look for a different role for herself. She remained behind, forgotten, in the same state as when people began to turn away from her. None of the innovations of the ages entered her obdurate walls. She locked herself away, heard nothing, saw nothing, and allowed nothing to enter in. After I had been in Vienne for three days, it struck me as peculiar that I had traveled there by train. Strange, almost unaccountable, that there was a station here, and that you sometimes heard the whistle of a locomotive. What were trains doing here? What did they have to say for themselves? This was where the dead lived! In these streets was no one who had anything to do with the world! Here people lived like monuments. Women sat at a window all day, and next to them sat their equally impassive cats. Dogs slept in the middle of the road, and no vehicles disturbed their sleep. There was one pedestrian, which was me. Behind the glass-bead curtains, which stood in for doors, nothing stirred. I stayed in Vienne thirteen days. When I arrived the women in the windows looked at me as if I were a ghost. When I left, they were still no wiser. The dogs were still asleep in the middle of the road, as they had been on the day I arrived. Were they really only asleep? Were they not dead? And were the old women really sitting by their windows? Or did they have the ability of the dead to see through the living as if they were air or glass? Had the inhabitants of Vienne even noticed my presence? Or had I been blown through the town like a breeze, which old people can barely feel and the dead not at all?

They unlocked a hotel room for me and let me stay there; in a shop they sold me bread and cheese and sausage, and they acknowledged my greetings with a faint nod. I was shocked wherever I went by the sound of my own voice. My footsteps were remote sounds to my ear. And each time I stopped in front of one of the monuments that the guidebook expressly instructs the visitor to see, I didn't have the sense of seeing some witness of a bygone age; no, it was like seeing a contemporary. And even though the monuments were from different historical periods, they all shared the same quality of otherworldiness, just as in another life the differences in age between fathers, sons, and grandsons are removed and all the dead are the same age. The Gothic church was the sister of the Roman temple.

In other cities, living cities, you learn to tell from the present day—which will in time give birth to tomorrow and the day after tomorrow—how much yesterday is different from the day before yesterday. But in Vienne the present was already past. There was nothing new by which I could judge what was old, and what was older yet. And all at once I grasped how little names, types of architecture, style mean. I took in everything past with an equally loving eye. Were the different forms supposed to demonstrate the oppositions of various peoples and nations? In essence all these constructions were the same: in their pure lack of aim, which is at the same time the highest aim of all: to reach God. Even the flat Roman roof was upraised like the palm of a hand; the Gothic arch was like a crooked index finger; the temple was hewn from ever-lasting stone, from everlasting stone the church.

The different styles were no more than different games with different rules. Just as children keep inventing new games, so the different peoples kept inventing new styles of architecture. And just as a child goes from one toy to the next, so I went from one piece of architecture to the next: First I stood in front of the Temple of Augustus; I stood before the ten shallow steps and sent my gaze up them; I got to the columns, which are no walls but pillars for walls of air and sun; saw the daylight cautiously lay the shadows of the columns on the tiled floor, carefully, as if the shadow of a column were also a fragile thing; saw the triangle at the front under the gable, which is like a forehead and like a large closed eye. Six columns cast six shadows. So there were twelve columns. And each of these few columns seemed to redouble itself. Soon there was a small, regular plantation of them. At the back, behind this wood, was the door that kept the holy of holies. Should I ask to have it opened? There was no attendant. Who could say if there was a key? Perhaps there was no key. When the Divine Augustus left the temple, he locked it and took the key away with him. In other cities these doors were broken open. Not in Vienne.

I will never set foot in the temple. If I were to stand in it, I would see that it is empty and that the locked door keeps nothing concealed, no statue, no godhead, no worshipers. The door was locked on nothing, on the past. The temple contains exactly what I can already sense outside, and what would come as no discovery if I were to get inside. What is there is waiting. I can feel it waiting behind the locked door. This is the only place where anything is still waiting. The temple is the only intact Roman building in Vienne. Only one wall of the old theater survives. And then there are the ruins of an old staircase that once linked the forum to the palace. The remains of the forum form part of a medieval court-yard in which a few ancient people still live. The stones of the old form went into a newer form, just as one epoch flows into another. Here, I feel movement without definition, without edges. The stones go by like the hours.

It was 58 B.C. when Julius Caesar had the huge aqueduct built. Roughly five hundred years later, Gondebaud, the king of the Bur-gundians, entered the city via the aqueduct, and conquered it. The monument was a conduit for history. As once the water, now a new epoch was entering the city.

Only the monuments to the gods are intact. As the Temple of Augustus remained unscathed by the years, so the cathedral. Shal-low steps lead up to it too. Its towers lie recessed behind three arches, like eyes behind wild, prominent eyebrows. On each arch are sixteen hollow crowns of silvery white stone. In each crown lives a pair of pigeons. The birds come and go, fly up and return, like fluttering prayers. Over the portal the arch extends over six columns of a second, high, unattainable portal. No earthly wor-shipers come here. This is the angels' entrance.

Within is the resting place of the cardinal de Montmorin and the cardinal de la Tour d'Auvergne. Old women sit in the hollowed-out chairs and pray. The ceiling is a dark blue star-spangled sky. It is so alive, so real, that you might suppose it was the original version of the night sky, and not the other way round. Happy the worshipers who pray here! They get to see their prayers rising straight up and reaching the stars. In this church every prayer must be granted. The heavens are so near that they must hear the soft-est beseeching. Only, there are no living people. The prayers of these people are free of all earthly torment. Their wishes are already those of another world. Heaven is so low here because they are so close to heaven.

High up on the hill, under stone crosses, lie the authentically dead. From time to time a tiny, ancient old woman will wander up there, with a candle, a flower, or a stick in her hand. It doesn't look as though her purpose is to visit the dead. Rather it looks as though she's going out to lie down in a grave herself. Her second home on the hill has long been booked. Down in the town she has only an old cat, a grandfather clock, a pair of knitting needles, and a plaster Christ.

I was in Vienne thirteen days. I would go to the post office to get a sight of a living human being. In the evenings I would go out to see the workers coming off shift, to hear some loud voices. The workers were silent. Most of them lived outside town. In the post office the counters were asleep. In the evenings a few children would be playing on the street. But they weren't like children in other cities. No dog barked. The bells rang out from the church towers, but not like metal bells, more like a heavenly summons. A policeman whisked through the streets on a ghostly bicycle. A prison warden lived in a prison without inmates. All the doors were glass beads. All the windows were open. Foreign tourists came driving in in automobiles, sped through the city, broke into the silence of the cathedral, ran their eyes over the Temple of Augustus, and drove on.

Twice in the night a locomotive wailed like a human being.

15

Tournon

I didn't take the train to Tournon, I walked. It took me three days. I walked along the Rhône, without a map, without a guide, and without stopping anywhere for longer than a single night. I saw the dark boatmen on broad rafts and heavily laden barges, and the anglers, as taciturn as the fish that so rarely permit themselves to be caught. Always I had the roaring of the river in my ear. The farther it flows, and the closer it comes to its destination, the nearer and louder and more dangerous it becomes. It's had enough of shipping, and it doesn't like bargemen. And yet it makes a sweet melody when you walk beside it, and its voice is softer than its character. Many French poets were born along its banks. Rivers do more than irrigate the soil. Wine grows on the slopes, and poets flourish. The troubadours sang here in the Middle Ages. A few miles on, not far from Avignon, is the magical castle called Les Baux, the white castle of poetry. If Tournon hadn't been here, I would have walked on day and night to reach Avignon, the whitest of my cities. But here already rise the fortress walls of a medieval, a Romantic, almost a German city: I mean Tournon.

Have I not just come from Vienne, which never stopped being Roman, even though the Burgundians conquered it, and it became the city of the German emperors? It's only three days, and yet I feel as though I'd walked through whole centuries, froth-full of wild history, that lie between the period of Roman hegemony and the period of the hegemony of Latin. The triumphal progress of the language was more glittering, more significant, and of greater duration than that of the people. The world was transformed, and people were still and again speaking Latin.

As I reached Tournon it started to rain. Ahead of me loomed the jagged walls of the ruined fortress, and I thought I could see no way into the town other than to scale these perilous walls. Nowhere was there a gate, nowhere a path. High above me I saw dripping bars in front of murky windowpanes. A couple of steps led into a narrow lane whose end you could see a long way off. It was a dead end; it ran, not knowing where it was going, slap into a wall that to my eye was even smoother and sheerer than the outer walls of the town. No one lived there. Anyway, why would people live in a street that you don't know what it's there for? Streets are there to connect. They lead the living to the living. This one, though, led the stone to the stones.

In the distance, muffled by the sound of the rain, I heard voices, the whinnying of horses, and the bright, chiming, calming clang of hammered iron from a blacksmith's. Not many sounds are capable of reconnecting a solitary wanderer so instantaneously to life and human fellowship as that. The ring of a hammer on iron is like the voice of a deed, and like a bell it summons us to some common purpose. As though the hammerblows had told me the way, I suddenly noticed another little path, a lane, narrow as a bottleneck. It led me up into the town.

I love finding myself in the broad centers of towns, those squares and places from which the streets radiate out in different directions, so that they are not only a center but also a beginning.

These squares tell you the character and the disposition of the town. They may be quiet, quieter than other parts of the town, or again they may be noisier than any of the lesser streets. They may be hallowed and tucked away, noble and proud, or the focus of life, filled with noise, working and purposeful.

Tournon had no center. Tournon consisted of streets that were inextricably tangled up with one another. A horrible panic seized me: I haven't just come to a strange town. I've landed in a strange century. I want to get back to my own time. And just as a facile bit of folk wisdom, easily refuted by one's waking brain, may, in the context of a dream, become full of a looming and substantial truth, and oppress us, so all at once the phrase "darkest Middle Ages" took on a dangerous life, and started really to frighten me. I want to get back to my own time! Never mind that it's full of dead knowledge and runs on stupid machinery! I am a child of my time, a part of it; I am in the present. And never have I felt so much a part of this century, never was I so stirred by the thought of a spacious avenue, an automobile, running water, airplanes. In the space of a second, you can feel an unfathomable consciousness of time. With alert senses, in broad daylight, you can fall out of your own time, and stumble around among the centuries, as if time were space and a historical age were a country. That's what happened to me in Tournon.

On the one side, hills; on the other, the river. There's no room to breathe. The houses are ensnared. They can't escape. A whole town has been trapped. It is protected from the enemy but only in the way of a man who no longer needs to fear anyone for the simple reason that he is behind bars for life. Effortfully a street clears a little space for itself. Oh, it encounters a wall, it tightens its belt a little more, holds its breath, squeezes its way through, and there it meets a sister street in exactly the same position. Like crooked worms, the streets wind in and out of the houses. And the houses in turn are pushed toward the river and would certainly drown if the blunt fortress wall didn't hold them back.

I walk right and left, forward and back. I hear people speaking, and I see their movements, and everything is remote from me, as though separated by a wall of glass. A child laughs, but it's not the laughter of a child of my time. I am able to feel at home in other countries, but not in other times. Our true home is the present. This century is our fatherland. Our fellow citizens and our compatriots are our contemporaries.

Were it not for the celebrated lycée, founded by the celebrated cardinal of Tournon, I would certainly have plunged out of Tournon, back to the river, across the suspension bridge to Tain. There there is a station. There are trains to take me back to the present.

The monument to the cardinal, a small bust, is placed modestly outside the lycée, at the left-hand corner, not in the courtyard, not in front of the main entrance. As if the wise cardinal had put it there himself! Oh, what prudent self-restraint! How worthy of Jesuitical tradition! And what a face! Who are you? Cardinal, courtier, monk, scholar, womanizer, man of faith, skeptic, judge of character, misanthrope? When I look at your little eyes; your long, thin, slightly shriveled-looking lips, your small but pronounced chin; your bony nose that still seems to vibrate in the stone, then I believe you were set on appearing to be everything to all people and keeping your true nature a secret. You were no scholar, because you had a career. You didn't have ideals, because you were ambitious. Heavenly immortality wasn't enough for you; you wanted the earthly kind as well. Whether you ever had the former, I can't quite say. But the latter is assured you. Even today your lycée is a school that is attended by more than a hundred pupils, and every one of them takes your name into his life and hands it down to his children. The future is with young people, so you were right to found an educational establishment, rather than, say, an old people's home or a hospital!

The lycée is on vacation. The evening sun is in the corridors, the windows are open, the concierge is wiping the dust off the desks, only the school secretary is in his office, processing applications. I feel like going in and applying. Oh, but I'm thirty years old! I'd like to be young in this crooked and medieval but white, white town, be a boy and play on the town walls and go out on the Rhône when I should be attending the cardinal's lycée. And then to emerge from those Middle Ages into the heart of the present— a step into life! How differently I would feel it! In how many centuries I would feel at home! And how alive it would be in my blood—the understanding of the continuing evolution of human history—how each century would be linked to the next in my soul, and how proud I would be to be human! The children of this country feel that we must continue and extend the work of our forebears if we are not to lose ourselves. Their youth has been put to the study of history. Immersed in the cultural understanding of previous times, they view contemporary developments from a braced and critical perspective. Nothing can alarm them the way it alarms us. It takes a newspaper headline to throw us off balance. Whereas that country took no more harm from a world war than sorrow and tears. It left us in turmoil.

Quite an extensive little town of its own, the lycée. The little chapel has the intimacy of a small classroom, and the young voices are still everywhere to be heard; and on the wall, behind the confessional, hundreds of pencils have scribbled foolish scribbles and written down girls' names, each stroke a secret emotion, not to be passed on to any father confessor but chalked up on the wall. How easy it is for me to read these, and how transparent their code!

It has long since stopped raining. The pink of a rinsed sky tints the windows and walls of the chapel and the face of the old concierge. That's a devout, heavenly makeup for old women.

In the evening the town sleeps, and the crooked, anxious lanes rest from their tireless flight. Now I go down to the river. Now I see the white half-round tower of the bastion, with the narrow black loopholes for archers cut into its body, and its tiny barred windows, scattered irregularly across the wall, behind which the convicts of Tournon do their time. But the mayor, the subprefect of police, and the prison warden are also to be found living here, behind these selfsame walls. Smaller, newer buildings press up against the tower; from a distance what you see is a clump of roofs, a freshly plucked and untidy bouquet of houses.

As white as this one tower, so white will all the towers of Avignon be. Tonight I'm going on to Avignon. Avignon you have to enter by day. Tomorrow I will be there.

16

Avignon

The aspect of the landscape changes sharply and often. Only the three basic colors remain constant: white stone, blue sky, dark green of the vegetation. But the shapes of the earth are subject to continual alteration. Here the hills are jagged and bleak, then they are round again, and soft. Here you get the bristle of cloven rock, and there already the smile of the plumped plain between gentle rises. The great Provençal novelist Daudet* made the very pertinent observation that the strong sun tends to exaggerate the landscape. Harsh light produces harsh shadows and a stronger contrast between light and shade. The sun reveals more details and gives them greater prominence. In pallid, foggy countries individual features tend by contrast to lose themselves, and it's as though the low and oppressive sky were pushing down on everything that strives upward. I realize I have only ever walked in foggy countries. My walks were a grappling with the unexplored recesses of the landscape. Through all its goodness I could feel

*Alphonse Daudet (1840–97), a popular French nineteenth-century novelist. Julian Barnes edited and translated the record of his excruciating suffering and death from syphilis (*In the Land of Pain*, Knopf, 2003).

nature's unreliability, which we anthropomorphize into something like "the imp of the perverse." Here, for the first time, I walked with joy. I could understand the carefree pleasure of people just following the road. They would not encounter anything scary. There was only one thing they lacked: the forest.

Yes, there is no forest here. They lack the sweet humidity and the secret song of the forests. Forests are where a landscape hides its secrets. This landscape has no secrets. Oh, I understand that they grow rationalists here, while mystics sprout elsewhere. The wind—the famous, hymned, and dreaded mistral—has nothing to stand in the way of its vehemence. Elsewhere forests know to detain the winds, wrap them up, calm them, as mothers do with big, strong, wild children. Here, there are no forests. Here are only gardens. Half of nature is privately owned. What rich country! Every second inhabitant has a huge sheer fortress wall round his property, crowned with horrid shards of glass. The walker should avoid getting tired here. He could only lie down in the dense, heavy, white chalk dust of the road. All the side roads lead to locked-up houses and fenced-in fields. I understand: Where nature itself is so kind, the gardens can be locked and unyielding. The sun ignites the sparse woods; one after another they burn down. The woods die, and still things aren't sufficiently clear and visible and focused in this country. Think how ruthless much-praised light can be, and how clement oft-scolded fog!

Avignon, though, could not lie between forests. Avignon needs light.

Avignon is the whitest of all cities. It needs no forests. It's a stone garden full of stone flowers. Its houses, churches, and palaces were not built, they grew. Their classic forms still have an organic secret. Its walls rustle like trees. Their stone is white and as endlessly tragic as anything infinite. Storybooks sometimes have descriptions of such cities. Simple devout people imagine a celestial city where the blessed dwell along similar lines. Boys dream of such cities, with broad white walls, a hundred bells, and flat roofs on which queens promenade.

When we think of a fortress we think of some louring and jagged castle behind beetling gray granite walls. But lo! here is a friendly, almost inviting fortress. It would be a pleasure to lay siege to it. One would admire it so much, one would forget to fight it. To conquer it, one would have to seduce it. No blood would flow here. No cruel deaths would be died here. The authoritative chiming of the bells would be enough to silence any tumult.

When I stood before one of the great gates that are set in the white walls of the fortress, like gray stones in a ring of silver, when I saw the flat crenellations of the towers and the noble strength, the aristocratic firmness, and the frank beauty of these stones, I understood that a heavenly force can indeed find earthly expression, and that it can even do so without compromise. I understood that a spiritual force is able to secure itself militarily without incurring any loss of dignity, that there is such a thing as a celestial militarism, which has nothing, but nothing, in common with the terrestrial kind. These fortresses were established by popes. They are religious fortresses. They are sanctified might. I can understand that they served peace. There are pacifist fortresses and weapons that serve peace and prevent war.

Is this a medieval or a Roman city? Is it European or Oriental? It's at once none of these and all of them. It is a Catholic city. And just as Catholicism is a cosmopolitan religion that embraces all peoples, so Avignon is the fortress of the Catholic Church, a cosmopolitan, organic fusion of all sorts of traditions and styles. It is Jerusalem and Rome, it is classical and medieval.

For five hundred years the most refined taste obtained here. For

five hundred years all sorts of artistic, political, and literary directions were convoked here. For five hundred years the intellectual
and social cream of Europe lived here. The indigenous people
here were Celts, deft, tough, and intelligent. But it was Phoenicians up from Marseilles, Orientals who had undergone Greek
training, who were the founders of the city. Many Phoenician families stayed here. They were traders. But traders at a time when trade
was heroic, and every transaction served not just a material purpose but also a historical one, broadening the horizon, establishing communications between people! What a time, in which
merchants were considerably superior to the nobility in terms of
true culture, knowledge of the world, and farsightedness, and when
it took more courage to make a deal than it did to go to war!

At such a time was founded the city of Avignon, a city of heroic
seafaring trading people. Over time Phoenician blood mingled
with Celtic, Roman, Gallic, and Germanic. But it didn't disappear.
Even in the Middle Ages, the people retained the open and questing minds that are an inheritance of the Oriental- and Greek-edu-
cated seafarers, and in the capital city of the Church there ruled a
joyful Catholicism that was tolerant of a cult of Dionysus without
losing any of its faith and prestige. Even today the inhabitants of
Avignon are half Phoenician: noisy, enterprising, quick-thinking,
ready reckoners and cosmopolitans.

The history of Avignon proper begins in the twelfth century. The
oldest constructions that we see here today were built then: the
cathedral, and the even earlier bridge of Avignon, that was begun
in 1177. It was designed for foot and horse traffic. It was nine hundred meters long, but only four meters wide. In the thirteenth century part of it collapsed. Today only half is left standing. Its last
support rests on the little island in the river. I have seen an old colored engraving. It shows the traditional town dance on the bridge.

Even though it was so narrow that a clumsy turn could prove fatal, this was the dance floor for the people of Avignon. It moves me that the people came here to dance, on this narrow and dangerous spot. They can't have done it deliberately, probably it didn't even cross their minds, the fact that they were dancing, quite literally, on the edge of the abyss. They were mocking death. They skipped and reeled over the water. Their merriment was reflected back in the merry waves of the river, and from the water they borrowed their own good cheer. The old engraving showed children, householders, women, beggars, and monks all taking hands and dancing. What a commotion under the church's aegis! What a party under the eyes of the watching popes! Anyone who knows Daudet's lovely story about the "pope's donkey" will understand how popular the pontiff was on the streets of Avignon. Here, by the river, the Vicar of Christ strolled about and smiled. It wouldn't have taken much, and he would have joined in the dancing.

Because the popes were here on vacation. History is rather pompous about their time in Avignon: the Babylonish exile of the papacy, and so forth—but it was the merriest exile the world has ever seen. "Rome," writes Renan, "was in fact the most turbulent of all the Italian Republics. Its outskirts were like a wasteland, dangerous to any traveler. Being in Rome was an unendurable captivity for the Popes." Clement V left for Avignon. His successor, John XXII, began the building, started work on the fortresses, which were improved and almost completed under the time of Benedict XII. In addition the popes built three large churches in Avignon: Saint-Agricol, Saint-Pierre, and Saint-Didier.

The most enduringly impressive historical edifice is the palace. It was almost totally destroyed on the inside in the course of the French Revolution. Subsequently it was pressed into service as a barracks for a long time, almost up until the war. The military authorities were most unwilling to vacate the palace. The inside, accordingly, is bare, with gray cracked whitewash plastered over the walls. The restoration, which was begun a few years ago, is proceeding very slowly. Twice a day groups of tourists are shown around it, and it is the subject of misleading explanations which a guide gives visiting Americans for a tip.

But nothing that was done in piety—that was created for a different immortality than is available here on earth—can ever be completely destroyed. Pay no attention to the guide! Leave the main herd of tourists to go where they will and look at the "*Fenêtre de l'Indulgence*," which is like a gateway to the kingdom of the sun, supported on four columns and forming five slender portals under a surprisingly pointed arch, in which a large, circular ornament is bracketed by two smaller ones, like a heavenly flower; a wheel with living spokes, curved crosses of light and glass; a round resting place for the light of day; the sun trapped in an artful net. For a moment I stop at the end of the great gallery which is long and narrow, whose ceiling gives birth to a hundred arches, an arch every second or two, like a curtain of swagged stone, as various and animated as soft drapery, and seeming, by its subtle reflections, to give the illusion of infinity. A small strip of sunlight breaks through at the end of the corridor, and behind that square islet made of light, and gold, silver, and twirling dust particles, a staircase leads who knows where, perhaps straight to heaven; innumerable, small, narrow, steep steps, with no respite and no pause, like a scurrying little ladder.

Then I am standing in a courtyard. It is enclosed on all four sides like a gemstone. There are many black gates set in the walls, but they don't give the impression of leading anywhere. In this courtyard a prisoner would feel his helplessness more than in the smallest, darkest cell. He might be able to look in at a window, but he

could never look out through one. There is a well, choked with
many feet of sand; there are wooden blocks and a few boards and
posts. And yet this is a courtyard in a palace. Wonderful windows
give on to it. Soldiers had target practice here, and drill. They used
to prop their rifles in this archway. Strange, the barracks yard
where I was taught to "shape up" didn't look anything like this. Is
there not some sacred influence vested in a stone, a pane of glass,
a piece of carving, that can save a courtyard from utter desecration?

The military authorities didn't know what they were doing
when they had the tender murals that were here painted over.
Under the weak but effective protection of whitewash, they survived for many years. They were right, the military authorities.
Such pictures are deleterious to morale. They were no fit sight for
men exercising. Whitewash, whitewash, whitewash! Cover over
the frescoes of the Crucifixion by Matteo Giovanetti de Viterbo.
Christ has the leanest and puniest arms, his body is no thicker than
a leg, his pierced palms are curling inward but still open and facing the onlooker, as though still giving even in death; the eyes are
closed as in sleep; it is the second after death, there is no more pain
in the face, only a quiet satisfaction; the poor, protuberant knees
seem to stick out, and the toes are shapely, elegant, long as fingers.
That's no picture for military men, nor is the fine head of John,
with long, luxuriant hair and beard, naively wrinkled brow, and
clever, bitter, kindly eyes, less a saint than a grandfather who has
been around and knows what's what, an evangelist for pious children. And nor were the recently discovered hunting scenes any
more suitable for warriors, even though hunting counts as a manly
activity. But the hunting in these pictures is nothing the military
authorities would have any time for. Because the trees, the hunts-
men, and the animals are all not of this world; it looks as though
the animals are still alive, even if they have been slain. They are

flat, glued to the wall; they are two-dimensional beings; they cast no shadows; they come from dream and will remain dream forever; one can't even be sure that they've been painted by earthly hands with earthly colors. Leaves, narrow, flat, still, as though molded in gold; noble hounds, with delicate, curly, ornamental tails and slender, flat heads, lean bodies on frail, loping legs. It is unreal, and of the deepest truth that comes to us only in dreams.

The walls of the fortress have an irregular outline. They follow the whims of the rock. It is almost an act of humility toward nature. These were truly pious builders. They wanted nothing more than to fortify the town. They were not striving for beauty. But beauty blossomed out of functionality. It sprang from the pious mind of the architect. He was building against hostile people, and to the glory of God. Never has a fortress become a song of praise quite like this one. God permitted the white stone to grow. Never will it change color. It will grow ever whiter with the years, ever more hallowed, ever younger. Just as someone who prays for years on end will become ever more enraptured, more luminous, more otherworldly. Cathedral and palace are both built against the walls of the town. They are alpha and omega. In this way the walls form part of the palace and of the cathedral, an extension of the lordly and the holy.

Across the Rhône the popes had a summer residence in the country. Similar walls, a daughter-fortress, summery, a vacation castle. Villeneuve is a small town, an offshoot of Avignon, also laden down with old treasures. There I saw the marble Mother of Christ with two faces, a Roman echo present in the Christian story, and the ivory Mother of Christ with the baby Jesus on her left arm, with a Roman face, the baby too like a baby Roman, with a round head and curly hair. The eyes of the Virgin are lowered out of modesty. In the Chapelle de l'Hospice is the grave of Innocent VI, a little church all to itself. The coffin stands between straight-edged pillars that meet at the top in pointed towers. The whole tomb looks like a lofty stone crown. The coffin even wears a crown. It sits in the crown, and quite fills out the lower part of it.

Not one of the churches of Avignon, not even the lovely Saint Peter's, can bear comparison in terms of grandeur and holy splendor with the cathedral. Its wide round arches are of heavenly proportions, the light enters it richly and softly through its many windows, the altar lies completely in the light, and an incomparable atmosphere is created by the interplay of the light and the curved stone, by the way the shadow is saturated with light, and at the same time by the tempering of the powerful southern sun by the help of the shade: an even brightness, but also an even dark. You enter the church through a relatively low, modest portal, flanked by two columns that seem to melt away timidly into the corners. A plain door, an old, bleached painting above it. The road to bliss leads through such unostentatious gates, as in the whole castle, in all the rooms. Everywhere, the doors seem to want to hide. They are loath to impose themselves on the walls. Space, and the harmony of space, is the paramount concern here.

In the bookshops of Avignon they sell likenesses of Petrarch, who lived in exile in Provence, and who at the age of twenty settled in Avignon, the birthplace of his Laura, and went on to live and to sing in Vaucluse, and then, after the death of his beloved, moved to Venice, where he founded the city library. Out of gratitude he was given a castle to live in.

I don't much believe in chance. That the most famous woman of all time lived in Avignon is something that would hardly have surprised me after five minutes here. The women of this town have every right even today to be sung by the great poets, and more, to be loved by them. I have come to the conclusion that in regions where there is much mixing of races, it is the female descendants that gain the most in terms of attractiveness. It is an injustice that the women of Avignon are less noted for their beauty than the women of Arles. The female type I most often saw in Arles was the Roman-Provençal: mature, a little severe, with a long thin nose and thin lips, large eyes and pointed chin, heart-shaped faces, perfectly suited to be hymned enthusiastically by any poet but to be kissed with caution, and only with the full under-standing that a kiss will have consequences. The women of Avignon are different. There is no single dominant type. But all the young women are long-legged and lightfooted, and all of them, even the blonds, have that soft, olive skin that never tans and never reddens, and on which the sun, the wind, the rain, and even the passing of the years, have no effect. Yes, not even the passing of the years! For, even though the indecent assumption gets bandied about from man to man that the women of the South age more rapidly than northern women, in Avignon women in their fifties have sufficient charms to keep a man faithful and to give promise of a lively old age, which I, at any rate, prefer to a mild decease. Nor should that be any surprise. Love keeps you young, and a pleasure whose health benefits are something of an unintended side effect, and whose greatest part is in any case played by an emotional enjoyment, should keep you limber late in life. In Avignon all the girls are happy. In the narrow streets where all the families sit outside in the evenings, with children and dogs and cats and parrots and in-laws and grandmothers, I only ever heard laughter, and to me, going by, evidently a foreigner, they called out friendly greetings, and if one happened to have drunk a little more wine than usual, then he would ask me in. Even if his house pro tempore, was the street.

I read the section on Avignon in the *Lettres historiques et galantes*.

The author of that book is the astute Mme. Dunoyer, better known to literary historians for standing in a sort of stepmotherly relation to Voltaire than for her own writing. She was the mother, to remind you, of that Pimpette who was Arouet's* first love. Mme. Dunoyer, who was a well-connected journalist, had succeeded, by a mixture of force and guile, in breaking off Voltaire's association with her daughter. Voltaire scholars, accordingly, have little good to say about her, with Brandes being particularly harsh. But she was a writer herself. And when I read her, it brought it home to me once more that writers, be they men or women, should be judged on the basis of their style and literary talent rather than on their character and actions. Never, going on what I had been told of her, would I have guessed that Mme. Dunoyer would have written in such a fine hand. She describes life in seventeenth-century Avignon so vividly that I felt I was there in person. If one can believe the author, Avignon was then even a step ahead of Paris in terms of gallantry. Fashionable society loved to foregather there, the streets were thronged with smart conveyances, it was a *corso* for the most diverse peoples, nations, estates, and uniforms; you saw diplomats, cardinals, brightly dressed nobles. What most impressed Mme. Dunoyer, however, were the gold-bedecked Swiss Guards. She was, after all, a woman as well. And she won't have been the only one with whom those Switzers found favor. Each time I saw a powerful, broad-shouldered William Tell figure among the generally short, slight, boyish men here, I would think of the blessed effect of the pope's Swiss Guards.

Not for nothing did they stay behind so long in Avignon after the popes had returned to Rome. If I were the pope, I would be

galantes—Published in 1707. "Arouet" is of course Francois-Marie Arouet Voltaire (1694–1778).

here still. I would sit, which certainly couldn't be accounted a sin, in front of Delorme's portrait of *A Lady from Avignon in a Ball Gown* in the Musée-Calvet, and spend many hours marveling at that face, a childishly pert expression with outthrust lower lip, eyes directed upward, perhaps at some balcony or toward the blue Avignon sky, the delicate but firm arch of the eyebrows unambiguously raised but creating not a single little wrinkle on the smooth, round, fair brow. An undeniably conceited expression, a little skeptical, a little mocking, but for all that still childishly expectant. I would love that short but quite assertive nose, and the long upper lip with the delicate embrasure. A belle, certainly, and from the best circles: but still with something folksy or rustic about her; dressed differently, she could be a beautiful peasant woman. Because the "country" here doesn't coarsen its daughters, and I have seen maids with the softest hands in the world. It's a very cultivated soil, in every sense, a land with no corn, with no potatoes, without black bread. It produces healthy but high-strung people. I have watched the elegant self-possession of farmers' wives in their country finery eating in the best restaurants in town. Nowhere in Provence is there a gulf between city lady and countrywoman. To an old lady who had guided me in Les Baux, and who offered me two photographs of herself to choose between— every elderly person in Les Baux sells postcards of themselves—I replied that I couldn't decide, they were both beautiful in such entirely different ways. She immediately replied: "Oh, Monsieur, if you'd said that to me thirty years ago!"

If I were the pope, then, I'd live in Avignon. I would take pleasure in seeing what European Catholicism had brought about, the wonderful mixing of races, the colorful confusion of all the different essences of life, and how the results of miscegenation are actually not dull monotony. Everyone carries in himself the blood of five different races, young and old, and every individual is a world comprising five continents. Each can understand each, and their society is open; no one is forced to take up any particular position. This is assimilation at its best: A person may remain as different as he is and feel at home.

Will the world ever come to look like Avignon? The ridiculous fear of the nations, and of the European nations at that, that they might lose this or that "characteristic feature" and that colorful humanity might mix into a gray mush! But people aren't pigments, nor is the world a palette! The more mixing, the more characteristics! I won't live to see the beautiful world in which every individual can represent in himself the totality, but even today I can sense such a future, as I sit in the "Place de l'Horloge" in Avignon, and see all the races in the world shine in the features of a policeman, a beggar, a waiter. That for me is the highest stage of human evolution. And human evolution is what Provençal culture is all about, as witness the great poet Mistral, to some scholarly question regarding the races that dwelled in that part of the country, replying with bewilderment or asperity: "Races? But there is only one sun!"

17

Les Baux

The charmed world of little medieval epics of Romanesque-Oriental character may be depleted, but it has not entirely disappeared. Its home is in "the heart of Provence," the region around Maillane and Les Baux. I still remember the adventures of the knights-errant. Guided by a small, brightly colored bird, they travel through a dark forest, no more than a couple of miles across, suddenly to find themselves in a different country, with eighty castles rising up, the highest of them in the middle, and all of white stone. They ride over glass bridges, past rocks that are petrified kings, petrified trees, petrified lakes. In the castle lives the beautiful queen, a young widow waiting for a brave man to come by or the sweet, beautiful daughter of a cruel father. I remember that the trope of glass kept occurring. Either it was a glass lake that cracked open, and the knight found himself in a magic kingdom, or else he's asleep and in his dream he walks through a wall of glass, behind which the new and astonishingly white world opens.

When I came to Les Baux, I understood why glass comes up so much in the courtly romances of the Middle Ages. The air here is perfectly clear—like glass—and distinctly cooler than the pleasant warmth I felt only half an hour before. Up on these heights the mistral blows keenly on certain days; it gets trapped in caves in the chalk face, and in the hollow ruins and wide windowless rooms of the towers; it displaces the milder air and scours the atmosphere so you seem to see the rock behind a pane of glass and are surprised that you can put out your hand to touch it. Everything close moves away. Perhaps because you can't quite believe that it seems to be so close. Because you can't trust your eyes when, in the middle of a green landscape, a white chalk desert suddenly greets you. You don't need to be a naive knight-errant from the early Middle Ages to think you must have pushed through a wall of glass in your sleep. The mountains here are aggressive, and you don't come to them, they set upon you on your innocent progress. The broad road starts to climb more and more steeply. The rocks on both sides move ever nearer; already they are lining the road. Suddenly, one mountain rips the green cloak off his chalky, riven body, and then another does, and another. Now they are all bare. And now there are no trees, no bushes to be seen for miles around, only a frozen chalk sea, with rigid peaks and troughs, with stone ships and strangely congealed sea creatures. No shore, no edge, no land! The deep blue sky edges the implacable white on all sides, and the sun burns down on the chalk. But all this is no ice that might someday melt. It's all glass, glass, glass.

And this is where the ruins of Les Baux are.

They are not ruins in the accepted sense. Just the reversion of stone to stone. Chalk that once was a castle and now is chalk again. The whole castle was pitched on the rock. The rock had brought it forth, and dandled it on its lap for several centuries. Now the rock is rock again. It has started to grow again. It renews itself, and spills over the old outlines of the castle. And still people live in its intestines. The population of Les Baux numbers some three hundred souls. One hundred of them live in the ruins. Children are born and grow up between bleak stone and historical monuments. Young lovers traipse through caves in the evenings. They embrace on chalk. They conceive in empty graves. All the old people here become "guides." Outside every other door stands a man who wants to earn a tip from you. It's sad to see that the perspective-lessness of the desert has made the people perspectiveless also. How they all earn their living from pointing out a stone that you can see perfectly well for yourself. And no one can have any idea of what it means to have the splendid silence of history getting sixty dreadful holes knocked into it by the prattle of sixty guides.

Oh, people should be silent here—silent as the stone—and think that this castle was once the symbol of an epoch of human history. The overlords of the castle—they say it was the Hugues family—were once the mightiest powers in the land. They controlled eighty castles, and their days were considerably taken up with wars, sieges, and ambushing little merchants, but meanwhile their own beautiful wives were sitting at home, and it was in the wonderful period before "loving-kindness" became a hollow phrase, when it was a quality that women still had. The troubadours came to the castle of Les Baux from every side, they were the cousins of our German *Minnesänger*, but probably a little more amorous, and probably a little worldlier too. But all the fine words of love, and the whole baggage of notions that form part of it, were then still brand-new, had just arrived from the vernacular, and had not yet been sung to death. As late as the fifteenth century, a queen ruled here by the name of Jeanne, and delayed troubadours, wearing different costume and with new habits but still the old songs, continued to beat a path to this enchanted glass castle, which was so unreal and dreadfully white and louring, but in whose interior dwelled tenderness.

The only memorial to Queen Jeanne is the little Renaissance

pavilion that bears her name, and that Mistral sang so well that he was rewarded by a faithful copy of it, in which his mortal remains are buried. It's a little castle between two stone cliffs, with a little arched roof put together from mossy paving stones that looks like a tortoiseshell, with four little pillarets and a miniature gate, all a little the worse for wear, too much visited by tourists but moving in its warm, almost human modesty. More imposing is the Valley of Hell, a gorge some three hundred meters long, and still viewed by the natives with some trepidation. Infernal spirits are said to reside there. The stone there is even more jagged, the chalk still bleaker; it could be the gullet of a vast, fiendish crocodile. In some books it is stated as fact—with the self-assuredness that is such a dubious quality in historians—that Dante's *Inferno* was inspired by this valley. The only certain thing, though, is that Dante originally intended to write his great poem in the Provençal tongue. I was also shown the "Fairies' Grotto," which is mentioned in Mistral's *Mireille*. But in the vicinity of these ruins of castles, and of so much general strangeness, even a fairies' grotto can seem commonplace.

Not so the Church of Saint-Vincent, which dates from the twelfth, thirteenth, fourteenth, fifteenth, sixteenth, and seventeenth centuries. It seems that people who live in a stony desert look for relief in a house of worship, the way others would in a grassy meadow. All around, as far as the eye could see, they were surrounded by the stern, the hard-edged, the implacable. In this church blitheness flourishes. It is a wonderfully bright church, with fresh, healthy-looking, and life-affirming saints, with a lot of wooden ornamentation that still seems to smell of the forest, with low pews, as if for children, and an altar encouragingly near. When I visited the church, they were just getting ready for a local saint's day; the priest had his cassock tucked up and his sleeves rolled up his arms; children were carrying pine branches, women were beating rugs, infants were lying in cradles next to the poor boxes, the whole village was in attendance; the doors were flung open, the church's own brightness mingled with that of the day outside, there was an exchange of light in progress between two friendly and related worlds. I think the people who lived among those stones could have known no happiness had it not been for this church. Children who are born in caves first see the light of the world on their baptismal day.

In Saint-Rémy I went to see the famous mausoleum and the triumphal arch, two colossal Roman monuments, very famous and often described, impressive witnesses on an impressive scale, stone as durable as spirit, unimpressed by the centuries. Admittedly monuments here have an easier time of it than edifices in other countries, because it hardly ever rains, the sky is like a protective canopy, it tends to preserve and prolong rather than to shorten the life of whatever is set beneath it. Stones here enjoy a good and long life.

But it wasn't only looking at an old triumphal arch, a mausoleum, and the wonderfully preserved Roman theater in Orange that set me thinking about the Middle Ages and Les Baux. So what was it? Is it not elevating to witness the eternity of Rome, to be reminded of the youthful bloom of Europe, to be shown irrefutably that what's often forgotten lives on, and to learn that somewhere there are still stones that can prove what dull-witted men refuse to believe? Were these not stones with souls? Could I not still feel the road to Rome here? Down across the Alps, as undeviating as only roads with immutable and eternal destinations ever are. Fields and towns may have grown over it, but they can't get rid of it. Even little byways lead to Rome. Just like here, there will be the odd triumphal arch left standing somewhere, and even if they have collapsed, their massive, cool, stone breath will still touch anyone who can feel history.

And for all that, I can't forget Les Baux. Here, it seems to me, for the first time ruins prevailed over monuments. The monuments are lofty. But the ruins are tragic. In the dimensions of the triumphal arch, there is still the cheerfulness of a world that sings in victory. For all their colossality, there is harmony, not conflict. How they managed to close heathen eyes to the problem, and how easily and serenely their beautiful arches soared over ugliness and sadness!

But Les Baux is riven. The Middle Ages are tragic. Not because they were destroyed. If they had been preserved, it would have been still more tragic. Even the troubadours, whose arrival brought merriment, are tragic. The beautiful queen within her sheer walls, tragic. Death, birth, festivals, weddings, feasts—all tragic. The world was still naive but already anxious. Already the shadow of the crucifix falls quietly and sadly over the centuries. Pan's pipes still sound, but already the organ has started to intone.

It's no more than a few miles between the triumphal arch and the white ruins. The epochs are narrowly defined. The eras are separated by a step. Does it separate them, though? Is it a border? Not a transition? Do they not lie peacefully side by side, now that both have fought to an end? Did both not lie childishly side by side in the country where I grew up? Did the one in my dreams not flow into the other? Is there not one world again today, welded together by the force of memory? Does the Orient not survive in the Roman arch, in the medieval epic? Are there really distinct worlds? Is there not just one world? What seems to divide, to set apart—does it not in fact unite us?

No guide has the answers. We are here to ask. We are here to believe.

18

Nîmes and Arles

Alphonse Daudet is immortalized in marble in the little municipal park at Nîmes, in the middle of a small ornamental pool, in which two swans swim round and round, with the quiet precision and persistence of a pair of clock hands. Daudet is dressed in the somewhat flowing style that was thought to be poetic in the nineteenth century; for our taste it looks a little self-consciously arty, and the expression on his face looks a little too realistic in its pose of creativity, which the sculptors at the turn of the century thought of as a kind of purposeful reverie. If we are to believe Monsieur Falguière the sculptor, then Daudet is "musing." Even so it is a touching memorial to such a fine, quiet, and sensitive writer, who never left the confines of the bourgeoisie, even when he was poking fun at it. He was well able to laugh, and to make us laugh about this world of which he himself was a part, and still that world never took it amiss, though it was always very sensitive to mockery. Daudet is perhaps the only writer of his type whose fame is strictly confined to Western Europe. In the beautifully tended ornamental gardens of Provence, he is a cultivated bloom that has spread beyond its native bed but never outgrows it entirely. Maupassant, on the other hand, a northerner, was so scathing in his mockery that he still makes the French middle class wince today. It wasn't until 1925 that he had a memorial put up to him in his native town. He himself would have been quite happy not to have had one at all. Whereas Daudet has been on show in Nîmes in living marble since 1900, and is certainly modestly proud of his statue.

Because there is something conservative about the South it may be that it's easier in the South to be a real writer and a reactionary, to take the traditional lies of society for sacred traditions. The South conserves stone, conserves relics, conserves attitudes. The North is different there. In the North if a man fails to take on his society, he might still be a poet in the narrow sense, but as a writer—a mixture of a sage and a seer—he'll never amount to much. He might have something to sing about, but he'll never have much to say.

Anyone born in Nîmes and given his own monument fourteen years before the Great War can afford to be pretty pleased with himself. Nothing disturbs the bourgeois peace of Nîmes. Here they have even found a way to incorporate the great monuments left to them from the—distinctly unbourgeois—Roman period, and to set up an open-air cinema in the Roman arena. It never even occurs to the good people of Nîmes that more than centuries separate the arena and the cinematographer. They live unworried lives, and they weave together the different historical epochs with contented and insistent thoughtlessness, the way the blind weave baskets they will never see. They don't know what they're about, but it may be that they're fulfilling a great task. Theirs is the innocence that is sometimes given to people growing up in the shadow of history. They are like children at the foot of a volcano. To them the stone historical holidays are like ordinary weekdays. They treat the Emperor Augustus as a friend of the family, now deceased, someone with whom Grandpa used to play dominoes. Even with my own attitudes, which must appear highly inflammatory to these good people, I could happily live in their midst. It would take at least a couple of decades off my age. Together we could defend the arena from all attacks, even if I myself happened to be persuaded of their historical necessity.

Because I would feel sorry for all the treasures of the past, and I would wish that the new, and the coming, and the future man would keep some connection with the infancy of Europe, and with his own, or that, like me, he would find it. There must be, I think, some reservation, some protected zone somewhere, where the new may only enter without first destroying the old, with weapons lowered, and under the white flag of peace. These places would not all be geographically defined, but there are some that you could point out on a map. And southern Europe would be one of them.

I have learned here that nothing can continue to exist unless it represents continuity in some way—not necessarily linear or logical, but continuity. The chain does not break, nor may one break it. Thoughts and cultures do not vanish. Races do not vanish. In our midst—perhaps in every individual one of us—live peoples who seem to have disappeared off the surface of the earth: yes, but only the surface. To us now, facing our present storms, it may sometimes appear that a people, a race, or an epoch has breathed its last, and that elsewhere a new life, a new race, a new fight, a new victory, must begin. So much shortsightedness! In the very first cultural spasms of a long-since vanished race, yes, of a continent that has been swallowed up by the sea, may already be found, in final definition, our own very latest culture. There is nothing that is exclusively and entirely "the future," just as there is nothing that is irredeemably "lost." In the future is the past. Antiquity may disappear from before our eyes, but not from our blood. Anyone who has ever seen a Roman arena, a Greek temple, the pyramids of Egypt, or some crude Bronze Age tool will understand.

In Nîmes, as I say, all Roman memorials have undergone a sort of bourgeoisification. The Temple of Diana threatens to be a local assizes; the "Maison Carrée," formerly a Temple of Jupiter, a registry office (instead of the small museum it is); and the mighty amphitheater a court of arbitration. Nothing of scale, however venerable, can survive the dread spirit of petit-bourgeois contagion

And even though the amphitheater was built to house grisly events, and even though the bloody circuses of the Romans were an (albeit classical form of) outrage, an arena that now houses Provençal bullfights still has the atmosphere of a bourgeois casino. That's the most appalling side of bullfights: the way that the mere sight of the animal brings out the hero in the barber's apprentice, the tailor, the corporal. None of these people are professional bullfighters. In civilian life each of them is a petit bourgeois. But on Sunday afternoons he gets out his costume, and it may be that the possession of a colored rag to wave at the bull is enough to fill a henpecked and moneygrubbing farmer with real courage. He does put himself in danger, it's true. But the protective fence is ringed by little men in Sunday suits, men with little potbellies, and worried-looking weaklings, a humdrum reality and lack of ambition showing in their faces. And these people hurl their caps and insults at the bull, and tease and taunt him, and when he charges their fence, then all of a sudden they're not there. All of them are experts. All of them act as though they could grab the bull by the horns if required. And I see their mean, paltry little lives, which are as sour as their faces, their submissiveness toward anything that might represent "wealth" or "class," their swagger in the face of something helpless, their meekness in the face of strength. A peasant jabs a spear into the back of a bull—a peasant who, come tomorrow, will go back to haggling over the price of a pig: but he's a hero! Celebrated in the heroic songs of his country, the heir to bold customs, the bearer of venerable traditions, born on historic soil, and last but not least a petit bourgeois! A shy, timid, heroic, intrepid petit bourgeois. I shall never forget the fabulously white, endless oval of that arena. On the old stones—for which, as long as they were unoccupied, I had respect—sit the representatives of family life on Sundays in the south. The nobility of the bull in all this is like that of the stones. I know: There have been similar scenes before, when the gladiators called out their *Ave Caesar!* to the crowned murderer in the stands. But the people whose blood-lust was so insatiable, and who stacked these massive blocks of stone—they lived two thousand years ago! It seems to me that a generation raised on phonographs and newspapers, gambling casinos and baccarat, has no right to blood.

Not one of the poets of this country has had anything to say against these bullfights. On the contrary, many celebrate them. I am incapable of understanding either the patriotism or the genius that is blind to such beastliness.

There has been much scientific, historic, and poetical writing on the subject of bullfights. Each May, Provençal bullfights are staged in Paris. So why does anyone still wonder about the futility of the League of Nations and international law?

I was lucky enough to see the amphitheater in Arles on a day when they weren't torturing bulls. It was a quiet weekday. In Arles the old monuments have not been incorporated into the sphere of bourgeois life. They settled into the Arles of the Middle Ages and after. Early Christians hid in the "Alyscamps,"* and the medieval

---

*Ancient graveyard in Arles (the name is derived from 'Champs Elysees'), painted by Van Gogh in 1888.

inhabitants had themselves buried there. For a time they defended themselves in the circus against siege from without. But neither the living nor the dead took anything away from the intactness of the Roman edifices. They have something extraterritorial about them: the circus, which is even bigger than the one at Nîmes, no better preserved, but whiter, prouder, more sun-drenched; the remnants of the old theater with the two thin, stone pillars outside the semi-circle, still standing by some sacred chance, whereas round about everything crumbled and returned to earth; the small, round, faintly Oriental Palais de Constantin, ground level and on the roadside, like the house of a commoner, with three barred windows, where the iron is like a delicate weaving; and the "Alyscamps," of which not much survives; a broad gateway, with wide, room-size niches in the side walls; stones, busts, heads; and coffins, coffins, coffins.

In Arles the streets are so narrow that cars, carts and wagons are unable to pass each other, and one has to wait in a side street for the other to go by. But this is no accidental lack of space, as it is in Tournon, but a deliberately calculated one. Also there is a small, quiet, central square. It's quite green from the sunlight filtered through the trees, and the moss that grows everywhere. In this square stands Mistral, the great Provençal poet, in floppy broad-brimmed hat, walking stick and frock coat, with a goatee and sen-sitively flaring nostrils, a good man and a patriot. He started the famous Provençal museum in Arles: with a little erudition and a lot of poetic license, occasionally on panoptical lines, and with a naive pleasure in naive effects and childish tricks with the light. In one window, behind bluish glass, you see a room in old Provence, wax-work people, formed with historical and physiognomical accuracy, a resurrection in a dead material. You see weapons, cradles, good and bad paintings, letters, tools, objects handled by the great men of Provence; it's a very sincere collection, a family album of

Provence. There are very different and much older things on show in other museums in Arles: the famous copy of the famous Venus, busts from early Roman times, busts from early Christian-Roman times. The art historians have written volumes about them all.

I am surprised that the people of Arles have not absorbed any of the antique grandeur of the monuments among which they have, after all, grown up. They are quiet, discreet, modest people. They too, like the people of Avignon, like to sit out in the streets, but they talk in quiet voices, and they only have films screened twice a week. In none of the small towns of Provence have I heard such quiet, restrained evenings—twilight where nothing seemed to disturb the bells. Their sounds had the air all to themselves, and they wandered about in it for a long time before settling down to sleep.

The bells were those of the wealthy twelfth-century Church of Saint-Trophime. It has a splendid portal, which I could spend a long time gazing at. It seems always to be closed, as though this remarkable entrance couldn't possibly be intended for ordinary mortals. Seven white steps lead up to it. There is a pediment, supported on carved heads, and, below, a deeply recessed arch, of—as it were—multiply pleated stonework, hollow in the middle, and interspersed with small, round, slender columns, behind each of which four saints stand. They are under stone canopies, their heads are lowered and half in shade, they invite you to enter the church, modestly, in the way that saints would invite you. But no one passes through the double door, more held together than sundered by a column in the middle. It is closed, and perhaps it is only ever open on high holy days.

Through the churchyard is the way into one of the most famous cloisters in the world, dating back to the thirteenth century. A rectangular gallery frames the green, overgrown, and mossy rectangle of the cloister garden. Stone, sun, foliage, and damp are compounded to make that strange daylight we sometimes see in our dreams. The ceiling consists of very many, long, broad arches. Against the many double columns that separate the cloisters from the gardens rest figures of saints. Each saint has given a little nook to a pair of breeding swallows. Each one has a couple of birds to look after. It's green, damp, and yet still bright. It's a courtyard for old men who have no fear of death and are already longing for heaven, because this meditative cloister gives them a foretaste of the shady, green, and yet lightsome passages of heaven.

The whole town has something of the cool, old serenity of a cloister, and there is much vegetative stone and living marble. Walls, monuments, and fragments only come to life after a couple of hundred years, and with every further century that passes, they become more lively. Old walls, like old violins, acquire more sonority with every year. Arles is full of living stone. Its old scale—it was once dubbed the "Gallic Rome"—no longer shows. I keep being reminded of the fact that it was a colony of Roman veterans that Julius Caesar first settled here. Veterans might still be living here. This was where the local princes and, later on, the German emperors had themselves crowned. There is little left of the magnificence of a coronation town. Unlike Vienne, Arles did not suddenly die in full bloom. It faded away slowly. It has kept many memories, but they are basically foreign to the town. It's as though history had entrusted it with the keeping of an arena here, a palace there, a church and a museum somewhere else, but none of them were to belong to the town.

Arles, too, is a white city. But it is of the silvery whiteness of age, not the festive whiteness of everlasting joy. It basks in the sun like an evening, mossed with the green of many memories.

19

Tarascon and Beaucaire

In the pages of Mistral, there is a precise description of the wonderful feast of Tarasque. It is celebrated by the Chevaliers de la Tarasque. This order was founded by good King René on April 14, 1474. Among its bylaws are:

1. Most respectful maintenance of the tradition of the Tarasque games, which are to be held at least seven times per century.

2. The festivities, farandoles, and general jubilation are to go on for at least fifty days. No expense is to be spared in making the games as gaudy as possible.

3. Visitors are to be made welcome, and for the duration of the festival to be treated in such a way that they enjoy themselves, while their feelings and liberty are to be respected by all.

The Knights of the Tarasque process through the town to the strains of the Provençal march, drink, and eat a *tortillade*. On the Sunday before Ascension, the members of the order bring the ancient statue of the Virgin from the castle chapel, at the head of a long and festive procession. All the people of Tarascon, Beaucaire, Saint-Rémy, Maillane, and others towns and villages are present. The boatmen of the Rhône stand at the edge of the town with pipes and tambours, and welcome the Virgin. Just before sunrise on Ascension Day, the Tarasque is seen for the first time. It has the head of a lion, the shell of a tortoise, the belly of a fish, and inside this monster there are six men. Whitsun is the next great feast day, when all the members of the order sit together at a long table. The inhabitants of towns near and far attend the Church of Sainte-Marthe. There the banner and lance are blessed. On Whitmonday the festival proper begins. After Holy Mass the people parade through the town, with the knights of the order leading the way. The Rhône fishermen march behind the flag of Saint Peter. Then along comes the Tarasque. The knights face it in battle formation. The Tarasque breathes fire from its nostrils. Battle begins. The monster loses. And the knights march off, for a few more bevies.

This fabled beast, the Tarasque, is at home in Tarascon. She is very popular throughout Provence; her frequent depictions are exhibited in many museums and form a mainstay of the picture-postcard trade. The inhabitants of Tarascon call her "Grandma." That goes to show the sort of monster it really is. She is the dragon of the German and Slavic and Scandinavian world, but enfeebled by the southern sun and ridiculed by southern wit. Really she's an object of love and veneration, only fought for fun. Mythical monsters would do well to stay in the North, where the fog isolates them and magnifies their terribleness. When they come south, people lose distance and respect. The bloodiest, most murderous beasts become not just tame but ridiculous. And the heroism of mankind is no longer terrible and tragic but a rather boozy burlesque. Bloodthirstiness has become alcoholthirstiness.

Ever since I visited Tarascon and came across the story of the Tarasque, I think I've understood Tartarin. In this town, where seven times a century they fight a dragon who is a grandmother, at least once a century they produce a Tartarin, who does battle with tame lions and turns the whole of Africa into one big Tarascon. Here is the only form of heroism that is still tolerable among all the ghastly proliferations of heroism in recent time that have brought the whole idea into disrepute. Tartarin is the antithesis of heroism, simple as that. Long before all our concepts lost touch with their contents, Tartarin transformed the concept of the hero. Every hero in a way goes to Africa, and hunts tame lions. The greatness of this book isn't that it's created an enduring character, a "comic hero." No, it's that the idea of the "hero" has itself become comic.

Tartarin is an extension of the games of Tarasque. And the games of Tarasque are a consequence of this sun, which is so hot, that it melts the phrase, the cliché, before its true content can appear.

It speaks for the greatness of the book that it has made the town in its own image. All about me I see the Tarascon of Daudet, the Tarascon of Tartarin. It is a small, bright, friendly, good-humored, slightly pathetic, slightly funny town. Its leading citizens still go around dreaming of hunting lions. Even its railroad station is a little eccentric, as though devised especially for Tarascon. The entrance to the departure hall is upstairs. When you're standing downstairs, outside the building, there's nothing to tell you you're at the station. The road that leads into the town—and that actually makes up the town—is broad, leisurely, full of sunshine but not without shade either. Plain, white, single-story houses stand peaceably side by side, containing modest middle-class aspirations. And here is the corner house where Daudet's Tartarin lived. Lots of stout, self-confident men walk the streets, the successful heirs to the great hero. You can see pictures of Tartarin on hundreds of picture postcards on sale at every stationery and bookstore in town. The large window of the town's principal bookseller has the works of Daudet on show in various editions. How grateful the town is for its fame! Already the dark shadow of centuries of obscurity was looming over it, the shadow that sits on several towns with as great a history. Because, make no mistake, Tarascon goes back past Tartarin. In the Middle Ages it was the capital of one of the Rhône administrative districts. In the castle on the Rhône lived the brave noble lords. That castle today is a prison. But the Church of Saint Martha is as beautiful today as ever. It was begun at the end of the twelfth century, and so perfect did they want it to be, that they were still building it halfway through the fourteenth. It has some gentle and beautiful paintings, among them scenes from the life of Saint Martha, by Vien, Pierre Parrocel, C. Vanloo, and other masters. The seneschal of good King René rests in this church, in a magnificent Renaissance Italian coffin attributed to Franz Laurana. And Saint Martha herself, the patron saint of the town, whose body—so legend has it—was found in Tarascon, rests in the church. With these exceptions, the modest people of Tarascon have no other sights to offer. The whole of Tarascon is a sight. It lies there, like a successful, friendly, agreeable witticism among the lofty chapters of world history, a smile lost among notions of grandiloquence. It has no monuments. It has no arena. It has only Tartarin.

THE BRIDGE still stands, the one that Tartarin was afraid to cross. On the other side of it lies Beaucaire, which was once the greatest market in East or West. Every year it held the noisiest fair in Europe, from July 21 to 28. Here came Greeks, Phoenicians, Spaniards, Turks, French, Italians, and Germans. Rich Jewish merchants lived here. The most different bloods mingled here, and here was created the wonderful cosmopolitan mixture of races that characterizes the European South.

Yes, Beaucaire was a great and important city. Today it is gloomy, embittered, jaundiced, full of the sort of petty suspicion of foreigners that you tend to find among small traders in strait-ened circumstances. Here live the little descendants of the great merchants. Nothing so oppresses people as a celebrated ancestry of which they feel themselves to be unworthy. If it had been a city of nobles, of poets, of monuments, of science—then today it might wear the proud mourning of its lost distinction. But it was only a city of money. And today it has the miserable grief of someone who has lost a fortune.

Back to Tarascon, then, even though there's so little to see there! The *Schildastädte* of the north, of Switzerland, scattered over German and Slavic countries (there are a lot of Jewish-Slavic *Schildas*) have, in addition to their literary life, another, sober, busi-ness life. But in the South of France, no Schilda can permit itself to be Tarascon, and nothing more. Here they go out to fight their dragon-cum-grandmother not seven times a century, but seven times a week.

Tarascon is a heightened version of a Schilda. All Tarasconians have enough self-irony to appreciate that they are Tarasconians. Every Tartarin is his own Daudet. Every little shopkeeper sells caricatures of a Tartarin, who looks like his own brother. Where else can you find such pleasantness, flourishing at the side of irony? Where else can a man find the necessary equilibrium to be the butt and the author of the same joke? Here the bourgeois soul is like a seesaw, with absurdity sitting on one side and mockery on the other. It's the merry give-and-take of the old jesters' souls that you don't find anywhere else nowadays.

But think of the profound confidence and social rootedness it takes to permit these jests! How little of the convulsions besetting Europe they must feel here! How blissful the contentment of a world that seems so successful to itself that it waxes witty in its self-confidence, instead of crude or domineering, as we are used to in our climes!

There are no great Roman monuments in Tarascon. But I feel that the bright, witty spirit of the late Roman humorists is alive here, with its heathen twinkle. Only, the epigrams have put on weight, grown broader, slower, cosier. That's the Spanish and French influence.

Tartarin is the comic world, the opposite of the serious world, stuffed to the gunwales with history. He is the private face of officiousness. He is the hero in carpet slippers. He convinces me that there's a human being present, even under a suit of armor. Blessed be Tartarin!

20

Marseilles Revisited

Tartarin found Marseilles more perplexing than Africa. The difference between Tarascon and the countries of wild adventure is not so alarming. But Marseilles is a world in which adventure is commonplace and the commonplace is adventurous. You are allowed to find Marseilles perplexing. Marseilles is the gateway to the world, the threshold of peoples. Marseilles is East and West. It was from here that the Crusaders swam to the Holy Land. Through this harbor tales worthy of the Arabian nights streamed into Europe. Here Oriental motifs made landfall, here they dropped anchor, here they set foot on the soil of European literature and art. From here, centuries before the birth of Christ, the explorers Pythias and Euthymenes traveled up to the Baltic, and discovered Iceland. Marseilles is the heiress and rival of Carthage, the beautiful girlfriend of Rome, the Greek city, the "Gallic Athens." Here the Visigoths, the Lombards, the Saracens, and the Normans—all of them defeated conquerors—lapsed into Latin-Greek-Phoenician culture. Here the great Revolution was greeted with delight, here it found its second home, its real home, its words and its melody. Marseilles is the land of Pierre Puget and Thiers and—Edmond Rostand.

———

MARSEILLES IS New York and Singapore, Hamburg and Calcutta, Alexandria and Port Arthur, San Francisco and Odessa. Sugar, stearine, soap, chemicals, vinegar, brandy, porcelain, cement, and dyes are all manufactured in Marseilles. A tailor will run you up a suit in eight hours. In twenty-four hours a street may utterly change its appearance. In little wooden booths, on street corners, sit the scribes. It takes them half an hour to knock off a will or a marriage certificate, or to settle a court case. From wealth to poverty is less than a step. The homeless man sleeps on the palace steps. One shop sells food, the next love. The poor boatman's craft bobs alongside the great oceangoing steamship. Shellfish lie next to the jewelers' displays. The cobbler sells Corsican knives. The postcard seller does a sideline in snake venom. The cinemas in the old port are open all day long. A ship docks every hour. Every tenth wave washes a man ashore, like a fish. The Algerian Jew talks deals with the Chinaman in the café. The "dollar king" enjoys himself in a dive. Every other night there's a stabbing, a murder, a family drama. Life dances on the edge of a razor, which is a popular weapon hereabouts. Misery is as deep as the sea; vice as free as a cloud.

All sounds have the same rhythm. All sounds have in them something of the churning of the ship's engine. The bootblack solicits business by drumming with the back of his brush on the lid of his shoebox. Drumming also signals the end of his work. The streetcars and all the carts and wagons toot like automobiles. Everyone makes noise. Everyone beats the rhythm of the city. Everyone translates the music of the wave into his own language. The cry of the newspaper vendor is as imperious as a church's bells. And the churchbells aren't too proud to mingle with the profane sounds below.

The continuous mixing of races and peoples is palpable, visible, physical, and immediate. Royal palms stand next to proud chestnuts. The Rhône Canal takes you north and west, the sea south and east. There whistles the locomotive, here wails the ship's siren. Water rinses land, and land pushes into water. The darkest, narrowest lane debouches in the wide, shining boulevard. You can watch the enormous hands of history's clock moving. "Development" and "progress" are no mere words. You can see the foot of history and count its paces.

This isn't France anymore. It's Europe, Asia, Africa, America. It's white, black, red, yellow. Everyone carries his homeland underfoot, and the soles of his feet carry it with him to Marseilles. But all countries are blessed by the same near, hot, bright sun, and the one blue porcelain sky arcs over all nations. All have been brought here on the broad swaying back of the sea; all had a different fatherland, now they all share the one fathersea.

Here history doesn't leave any stone traces of its doings. It swiftly washes them away. Only the ghost of a past remains in its slipstream. Last week the Phoenicians were here, the day before yesterday the Romans, yesterday the Germans, today the French. Just as all the thousands of miles of the world can fit into a few square kilometers, so the ages press together here as if there were no room for them in eternity. Whoever doesn't believe in God feels the presence of some other force driving the centuries, and senses some deeper meaning in the randomness of their wanderings. In a simulacrum of the switch of ebb and flow—just as elemental, just as unarguable—the peoples come washing up, and they wash back.

Ropes on the waiting sailing ships make black threads against the blue sky. The new harbor is a city of ships. Oil floats on the sea's surface. There are so many masts that I can't see the sea. The smell on the breeze is not salt and air but turpentine. Oil floats on the water. Boats, fishing vessels, rafts, and walkways have been put down in such proximity to one another that you could cross the harbor and not get your feet wet, were it not for the possibility of drowning in vinegar, oil, and soapy water. Is this the boundless gateway to the world's boundless seas? If anything, it's the boundless supply of goods for the European market. Here are barrels, crates, beams, wheels, levers, tubs, ladders, tongs, hammers, sacks, cloths, tents, carts, horses, engines, cars, rubber tubing. Here is the intoxicating cosmopolitan smell you get when you store a thousand hectoliters of turpentine next to a couple of hundred tonnes of herring; when petroleum, pepper, tomatoes, vinegar, sardines, leather, gutta-percha, onions, saltpeter, methylated spirits, sacks, bootsoles, canvas, Bengal tigers, hyenas, goats, Angora cats, oxen, and Turkish carpets get to breathe out their warm scents; and when, on top of that, the sticky, oily, and oppressive smoke of anthracite swathes everything alive and everything dead, masks all smells, saturates the pores, fills the air, hovers over the stones, and finally grows so strong that it muffles sounds, as it has long ago dimmed the light. I was looking for the boundless horizon here, the bluest blue of sea and salt and sun. But the water in the harbor is dishwater with vast gray-green fatty eyes. I climb aboard one of the large passenger steamers and hope to catch a whiff of the distant shores the ship has come from. But it smells like Easter did at home, of dust and aired mattresses, of varnish for the doors, of laundry and starch, of burned cooking, of slaughtered pig, of cleaned chicken coop, of sandpaper, of yellow brass polish, of insecticide, of naphthalene, of floor wax, of preserved fruit.

There are at present seven hundred ships in the harbor. It's a city of ships. The sidewalks are made of boats, and the roadways are rafts. The inhabitants of this city go around in blue overalls, tanned faces, and large, rough, blackish gray hands. They stand on ladders; apply fresh brown varnish to ships' hulls; carry heavy buckets, roll barrels, sort sacks, toss out heavy iron hooks and catch chests; turn cranks and haul up goods on iron pulleys; polish, plane, clean, and create new disorder. I want to go back to the old harbor, where the romantic sailing boats stand at anchor, and the puttering motor boats, and where people sell fresh, dripping oysters for thirty centimes a piece.

The city shines white, it's of the same stone as the castle of the troubadours in Les Baux, and the Papal Palace in Avignon. But it's not ceremonial, it's industrial. It houses millions of wrecked lives. In Avignon, even the beggars are proud. In the old harbor of Marseilles, poverty is more than hunger. It's an unavoidable hell. Stacked up in infernal chaos, the human wrecks are piled on top of one another. Disease sends poisonous yellow flowers from blocked sewers. Mangy dogs roll around in puddles with children. Men in rags fight animals for discarded bones; thousands of men and women go around collecting dog ends; the dog lies in wait for the man, the cat for the dog, the rat for the cat, and all lie in wait for the same piece of putrid meat in the garbage.

The street of love has thrown off its official name, and bears no designation. No matter; people know where it is, and can find it if they need to. To go from the big cathedral to the old port is to hear tinny music playing incessantly from fifty phonographs outside fifty small, dingy stores. In front of the stores sit the women, the oldest and fattest women in the world. They sell bodies all day and all night. Men, coming off the ships, drift up the lane in loose groups of a dozen or so. On their way they peel off into the shops on either side. Then a phonograph will fall silent, a bead curtain falls in front of a grim gray sofa, and there will be a momentary space in the even line of women standing selling themselves out-side their doors.

There is nothing here but love and music. Some women hold little children on their laps. A lot of children grow up in this street, the saddest children of the saddest mothers. A music box plays beside their cradle. From the moment they first beheld the dark of the world, they have known the bed of venal love. The riddles of existence are supplied to them—and at the same time their banal solutions. Life lavishes its experiences upon them. The play-mates of their early years are sick cats, which are supposed to bring luck, and whatever the gutter will provide in the way of toys—a shell, perhaps, or a pebble.

Morning, noon, evening, night, all times of day are the same here. One can only see a thin strip of sky, and nothing of the sun. This love too is everlasting. The women who bestow it are ageless. Forty years ago, they were ugly and old. They could be young and beautiful for another forty years. Forty years ago, the music box cranked out the same melodies. For another forty years, it will continue to make divine music for the ears of insensate men. Forty years ago, it drove listeners away. It will continue to lure hearers for another forty. What is old, what is young, what is ugly, what is beautiful, what is noise, and what is music? If a day consists of many nights of love, and a night of love is a matter of moments? When the commodity is the woman selling it, and love is worth a dime, and a dime buys love? If night is a hardworking day, and sleep is a business?

THE RULES of the world do not apply in this street. With staring atropine eyes, made up to the temples, with false hair that never goes gray, with a dolled up age that has nothing in common with everlasting youth except stupidity, the women—all identical and therefore free of all feelings of rivalry—all stare at the same curb, the same cat, the same gutter—and the same man, whom instinct sends shoaling up the street in ten thousand versions. When a woman spreads her arms, the music box falls silent, because by a cunning mechanism, one machine is connected to the other.

Here everything ostensibly permanent is broken up. Here, it is re-assembled again. Here, there is continual rebuilding and demolition. No time, no power, no faith, no understanding holds for ever here. What is foreign? The foreign is at hand. What is at hand? The next wave will wash it away. What is now? It's already over. What is dead? It comes bobbing up again.

Even as I write this, Marseilles has changed again. And what I take a thousand words to describe is a tiny drop in the sea of everything that goes on, too small to be seen by the naked eye, hanging trembling on the point of my pen.

21

The People

What I like to observe in a city are its people. — STENDHAL

The first people to live here were the Ligurians. Red was their favorite color. The red was still there when the Phoenicians came, the Greeks, the Langobards, the Saracens, and the Visigoths. Red is joy. People in this country have never stopped feeling joy. It took the edge off the horrors of history. The barbarians did not long remain barbarians after they got here. Whoever came to this country with the intention of conquering it were themselves conquered. The peoples dropped mildly into the soil like seed. Harvest time came around. And what was harvested, time and again, was joy.

Before I came to the white cities, I attended a Provençal evening in Paris for Parisians and foreign visitors, an annual display of the old popular culture of the South. Provençal shepherds came with their womenfolk, paraded around the arena in a circle, with the pipe and drum players to the fore. It was a very simple, bright, merry march they played. The notes were soft, like moonlight, but they played it fast, with the sort of urgency that has nothing in common with stress or hectic. It was the kind of urgency that children feel when they're on their way to a party. And in between you heard the little drums, which were delicate, covered not with calfskins, as usual, but with fine silvery membranes. They marched in short, light, almost feminine steps. And yet they looked manly enough. They were healthy, good-looking people. The men in shepherd's costume of white trousers, colored waistcoats, black and colored jackets, and black hats with colored ribbons tied around them. The women in flowing dresses, little white lace crowns on their piled-up hair, colored bodices, high-heeled shoes. They were country people. Real peasant stock. Men and women who worked hard wherever they came from. But their movements were the inheritance of a long, rich, and well-structured line of ancestors. The women waited, bunches of red roses in their hands, for the men. One man after another raced up and received a bouquet from his lady, then defended it against all attacks from the other men. Even when beset by twelve knights, he always got away, his bouquet held aloft in his hand like a flame. He held on to it and delivered it to a safe place. Then he raced back to his lady once more, doffed his hat, rode away. Then the next man. And the next. Twelve times.

It seems that gallantry is a healthy reaction against whatever is rough in a society, and that the troubadours owed their existence to a rash of robber-knights. The courtly fight over a bouquet of flowers is as charming as a bullfight is revolting. Yet I had to put myself through the one to witness the other.

Happily, courtliness is more widespread in Provence than bull-fighting. People live well-ordered lives, civilization is long established, well founded, and widely and joyfully accepted. People have enough moments of tranquillity to be courtly. To see well-preserved monuments from a fabulously ancient past on a daily basis does give one a very striking feeling of security. You don't believe in sudden changes. Change does happen, but not suddenly. There are no storms. Nature and history don't work with surprise effects. Everyone has his own settled life. All the farmers own large estates of land. Every estate has a wall around it. The gates are left open. You can walk into someone's garden and take a nap. There is no theft, no one needs to debar anyone or secure anything. Everybody builds walls, not to shut themselves away but to show off the dimensions of his property. His wall symbolizes his power. But walls are heartless things. Even the beautiful white stone can make a man hardhearted. If you're sitting behind your walls, you don't see the starving beggar on the road. And by the time he's reached an open gate, he may have died of hunger in the lee of your wall.

There isn't much hardship in this country—and so you see more kindly faces than open hearts. Everything is passed on from generation to generation—the house, the silver, the morals. Children grow up who have never seen how much hunger hurts. They never will see it. Everyone owns a boat. It's not black, it's snow white. The potato, the manna of the poor, is little cultivated here. Everything is cheap. But if you don't have the money that is worth so little and so much, then you can't count on bread. Happy people love their happiness. And grief is so alien to them that hunger must strike them as suspicious. They are good people. But their goodness lies within them, deep and unused, like water in a forgotten well. No one draws on it. Nature does little damage. Sudden calamities don't cheat someone of their daily bread. The neighbor is a friend. But he will never be a brother. All dogs and cats are given food at others' tables. Unwanted animals are not killed. But there are a lot of stray dogs and cats. Everyone hunts and fishes. The people shoot small songbirds. They cut down woods. There are no woods left, and very little birdsong. The sun ignites some of the woods. The people don't concern themselves sufficiently. Good spirits live in the rocks. But the people have almost stopped believing in them. They remain true to their old customs. They wear traditional clothes and speak the beautiful, old, melodious Provençal language. Everyone loves his country. But it is not difficult for anyone to love this country. It's not at all hard to live here. You pluck love by the roadside. It grows as abundantly as the most delicious fruit. The earth is full of sap and juice. The bush will feed whoever needs. You can sleep in the open. But maybe some would like a roof? Everyone has enough sun. But maybe someone is crying for shade?

White stone, white stone, white stone! Olive trees among the white stone. But someone wants bread. See, the bread is behind high walls! Churches, churches, churches! Richly carved portals, rich paintings, golden altars. Everyone prays for his daily bread and doesn't know what it is not to have it. Everyone has his place, with name and date. His relationship with God has been regularized. His faith was rarely put to the test. His sins? The man who died behind the wall, he had no sins. Who can see through walls? Is it a sin to fence off your property? Is it a sin not to see through walls?

But how they love the helpless, the young, the weak! No yelling, no blows, no tears. No harsh father. Cats in every home. Soft, quiet animals with shrewd and forever alert eyes. Good corners, warm corners, quiet corners. High windows, deep recesses, sun, sun, sun. Old palaces, warm in the mild winters, cool in the hot summers. Stone floors, easy to clean, no mess. But few sewers, and those are dilapidated; the poor relieve themselves in the streets. Mighty arenas, holy temples, museums full of stone memories, tradition, faith. Slow to look to the future. How sunny is life! But how easy it is to be sunny! How remote is death, even with graves everywhere, even though every day old bones are turned up and new monuments discovered.

Much land is still unclaimed. Not enough inhabitants. The

ground is hungry for new seed. It has gulped so many different things, given back so many different things, now it is all one. It leveled them out. They will welcome strangers. On my way, which is northward, to the autumn, the fog, the forests, I see many go with me. They go without swords. But even if they did have weapons, they would set aside all aggression. Here life is stronger. Here they are not easily prepared to shed their blood. Here you find a childhood, your own and Europe's. Nowhere do you feel so easily at home. And even the one who leaves the country behind takes with him the best that a homeland has to offer: the memory of it, homesickness.

> *[From the corrected unpublished manuscript, probably completed by Roth at the end of 1925, after his journey in the South of France. It first appeared in the 1956 edition of his works, where it was confused with the* Frankfurter Zeitung *series of articles, and called "In the French Midi."]*

Part IV

The Wandering Jews

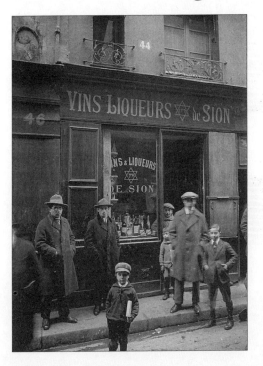

22

Paris

1.

It wasn't easy for Eastern Jews to make their way to Paris. Brussels and Amsterdam were both far more obvious destinations. The Jewish gem trade goes to Amsterdam. A few reduced and a few aspiring Jewish gem dealers found themselves compelled to remain on French-speaking territory.

The little Eastern Jew has a somewhat exaggerated fear of a *completely* foreign language. German is almost a mother tongue to him: He would far rather go to Germany than France. The Eastern Jew has a wonderful ear for foreign languages, but his pronunciation is never perfect. It is always possible to pick him out. It's a sound instinct on his part that warns him against the Romance languages.

But even sound instincts may be mistaken. Eastern Jews live almost as well in Paris as God in France.* No one prevents them from having their own businesses, and there are even whole ghettos here. There are several Jewish quarters in Paris, around Mont-

---

*A play on the German proverb *wie Gott in frankreich*, meaning "to live well" or "off the fat of the land."

martre and close to the Bastille. They are some of the oldest parts
of Paris. They are some of the oldest buildings in Paris, with some
of the lowest rents. Unless they are very rich, Jews don't like
spending their money on "pointless" luxuries.

There are some quite superficial reasons why it should be easier for them in Paris. Their faces do not give them away. Their
vivacity does not attract notice. Their sense of humor meets that
of the French part way. Paris is a real metropolis. Vienna used to
be one. Berlin will one day become one. A real metropolis is
objective. Of course it has its prejudices too, but no time to
indulge them. In the Vienna Prater there is almost no hint of anti-
Semitism, in spite of the fact that not all the visitors are fond of
Jews, and they find themselves cheek by jowl with some of the
most Eastern of Eastern Jews. And why not? Because people go
to the Prater to enjoy themselves. In the Taborstrasse, on the way
back from the Prater, the anti-Semite begins in feel anti-Semitic
again. There's no fun to be had on the Taborstrasse.

There's no fun in Berlin. But fun rules in Paris. In Paris, crude
anti-Semitism is confined to the joyless, the royalists, the group
around the Action Française.* I'm not surprised that the royalists
are without influence in France, and will remain so. They are not
French enough. They have too much pathos and not enough irony.

Paris is objective, though objectivity may be a German virtue.
Paris is democratic. The German perhaps has warmth. But in
Paris there is a great tradition of practical humanity. Paris is where
the Eastern Jew begins to become a Western European. He
becomes French. He may even come to be a French patriot.

---

*Anti-Semitic, right-wing neoroyalist organization founded by journalist
Charles Maurras in 1898, at the height of the Dreyfus affair.

2.

The Eastern Jews' bitter existential struggle against "papers" is less intense in Paris. The police are benignly remiss. They are more responsive to the individual case and to personal circumstances. The German police tends to think in terms of categories. The Parisian policeman is open to persuasion. It is possible to register in Paris without first experiencing three or four rebuffs.

Eastern Jews are allowed to live as they please in Paris. They may send their children to Jewish schools or French. The Paris-born children of Eastern Jews may acquire French citizenship. France needs inhabitants. It seems to be positively its duty to be underpopulated and forever to stand in need of new inhabitants, and to make foreigners into Frenchmen. In that lies both its strength and its weakness.

Admittedly there is anti-Semitism in France, even outside royalist circles. But it is not one hundred proof. Eastern Jews, accustomed to a far stronger, cruder, more brutal anti-Semitism, are perfectly happy with the French version.

And why not? They enjoy religious, cultural, and national rights. They are allowed to speak Yiddish as loudly and as much as they like. They are even allowed to speak bad French without incurring hostility. The consequence of such leniency is that they learn French, and that their children no longer speak Yiddish. At most they still understand it. In the streets of the Jewish quarter of Paris, I was amused to hear the parents speaking Yiddish, and the children replying in French—French answers to Yiddish questions. The children are gifted. They will make something of themselves in France, if God wills. And it seems to me he does.

The Jewish bars in the Hirtenstrasse in Berlin are sad, cool, and quiet. Jewish establishments in Paris are merry, warm, and noisy. They all do a thriving business. I sometimes eat at Monsieur Weingrod's. He does an excellent roast goose. He distills a good, strong schnapps. He entertains his customers. He says to his wife: "Get me the account book, *s'il vous plaît*." And his wife says: "It's on the table, *si vous voulez!*" They speak a truly wonderful mélange.

I asked Monsieur Weingrod: "How did you come to be in Paris?" And Monsieur Weingrod replied: "*Excusez, Monsieur*, why not to Paris? In Russia they throw me out, in Poland they lock me up, in Germany they give me no visa. Why should I not come to Paris, *hein?*"

Monsieur Weingrod is a brave man: He's lost a leg, he has an artificial limb, and he's always in a good mood. He volunteered to fight for France. Many Eastern Jews served in the French army out of gratitude. But Monsieur Weingrod didn't lose his leg in the war. He came home in one piece. But witness the role of fate: Weingrod leaves his restaurant and crosses the street. A car drives down the street perhaps as often as once a week. It chooses the precise moment when Monsieur Weingrod was crossing. It ran him over. He lost a leg.

3.

In Paris I visited the Yiddish Theater. Strollers were left in the cloakroom. Umbrellas were taken into the theater. The stalls were full of mothers and infants. The seats were not set in rows; they could be moved around. People wandered up and down the side aisles. One person left his seat, someone else sat down in it. People ate oranges, which squirted aromatically. They spoke aloud, sang along, applauded in midscene. The young Jewish women spoke only French. They were as elegant as Parisiennes. They were beautiful. One might have taken them for women from Marseilles. They have Parisian gifts. They are cool and flirtatious. They are gay and matter-of-fact. They are as faithful as Parisian women. The assimilation of a people always begins with the women. The play was a comedy in three acts. In the first act the Jewish family in a small Russian village wants to emigrate. In the second they get their passports. In the third the family is in America and has become rich and vulgar. They are in the process of forgetting their former home and their old friends, who have followed them to America. The play offers plenty of opportunities for singing American hit songs and old Russian-Yiddish songs. When the Russian songs and dances were put on, the actors and the audience wept. If it had been just the actors, it would have been kitschy. But when the audience cried too, it was genuinely sad. Jews are easily moved—I knew that. But I didn't know they could be moved by homesickness.

The relationship between stage and audience was close, almost intimate. For Jews it is a fine thing to be an actor. The director came out and announced the next production. Personally—not in the press, not by posters. He said: "Next Wednesday, you will see Monsieur X from America." He spoke like a leader to his followers. He spoke plainly and wittily. They understood his jokes. Almost got them in advance. Sniffed the punchline.

4.

In France I was talking to a Jewish artiste from the old Russian-Austrian border town of Radziwillow. He was a musical clown, and he was very successful. He was a clown by conviction rather than by birth. He came from a family of musicians. His great-grandfather, grandfather, father, and brothers had all been Jewish wedding musicians. He was the only one who had been able to go and study in the West. A wealthy Jew supported him. He was accepted at a conservatory in Vienna. He began to compose his own music. He gave concerts. "But," he said, "What business has a Jew got to be making serious music for the public? I've always been a clown in this world, even if they give lectures on me and a bespectacled newspaper critic sits in the front row. Should I play Beethoven? Should I play *Kol Nidre*?* One evening, as I was standing up on stage, I burst out laughing. A musician from Radziwillow—who was I trying to fool? Should I go back to Radziwillow and play at Jewish weddings? Or would I make myself even more ridiculous if I did that?

"That evening, it dawned on me that there was nothing else open to me except joining a circus, though not to be a bareback rider or an acrobat! That's not for Jews. I'm a clown. And from my very first appearance in the circus, I've been utterly convinced that I haven't broken with the tradition of my forefathers at all, but that what I am is what they should have been. Admittedly seeing me would have come as a shock to them. I play the concertina and the harmonica and the saxophone, and I'm hugely relieved that people don't know I can play Beethoven.

"I'm a Yid from Radziwillow.

"I like it in France. Maybe the world is the same all over for artistes, but not for me. In every city I look for Jews from Radziwillow. In every city I meet two or three. We get to talking. There are a few in Paris, too. And if they're not from Radziwillow, they're from Dubno. And if they're not from Dubno, then they're from Kishinev. And they're doing well in Paris. They're really doing well. Surely not all Jews can belong to the circus? If they're not

*Ashkenazi melody for the Day of Atonement, popularized by Max Bruch's cello variations of 1880.

with the circus, they have to toady to all sorts of people they don't know and don't like. They can't afford to be on bad terms with anyone. I just need to be a member of the Performers League. That's a big plus. In Paris, Jews live at liberty. I'm a patriot; I have a Jewish heart."

5.

Every year a few Jews from the East arrive in the great port city of Marseilles. They've come to board a ship. Or they've just disembarked. They were on their way somewhere else and ran out of money. They were forced ashore. They drag all their luggage to the post office, while they dictate a telegram and wait for a reply. But telegrams don't always get answered promptly, least of all those that ask for money. Entire families sleep in the open.

A few, a very few, stay in Marseilles. They become interpreters. Interpreting is a Jewish calling. It has nothing to do with translating, say, from English into French, from Russian into French, from German into French. It has to do with translating the stranger, even if he hasn't said anything. He doesn't have to open his mouth. Christian interpreters might translate. Jewish ones intuit.

They earn money. They take strangers into good restaurants and out into the villages too. The interpreters take a cut of the profit. They earn money. They go down to the harbor, they get on a ship, and they go to South America. The United States is difficult for Jews to get to. The quotas were usually exceeded long ago.

The Wandering Jews, 1927 (Norton edition, 2000)

Part V

Parisian Paradise

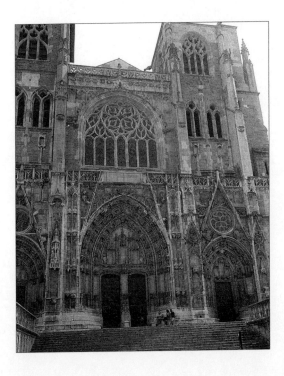

23

Count d'Orgel and
The Devil in the Flesh

Two Novels by Raymond Radiguet

O nly two novels were completed by Raymond Radiguet,[*] whose early death was much lamented in France and by some German admirers. *Count d'Orgel* is a love story that isn't a love story. In point of subject matter, nothing happens in it. It's a spring without a summer. Or an early spring that's broken off. Things flower and don't fruit. Things seed and don't flower. Something happens between a young man and a young married woman, but nothing serious. All the phases of this burgeoning relationship are recorded very precisely, as it were in slow motion. Inaction, through so much precision, becomes the heart of the action. The relativity of the "event" is clearly felt. The "happening" is there before it has even happened. The adventure that doesn't take place is as gripping as only the most exciting of thrillers.

The Devil in the Flesh is about a real, or should I say, an actual love affair between a very young man and the wife of a serving soldier. Rarely in European literature has a first passionate love affair been so implacably set down. Writers always preferred to surround the naked flame with rustling, pious branches. "Soulful-

---

[*]Raymond Radiguet, author (1903–1923).

ness" always had to be part and parcel of desire. Here there is only passion, only blood, only life. This one volume is enough to put thousands of volumes of superfluous and mendacious love poems out of business. It is a burning idyll. All around is the world war. Its murderous sound even penetrates behind the lovers' locked door and fills the hour in which the blood speaks. In this way it is a war novel too, though set in the hinterland. Because a true writer, even if his story is somewhere far away, will not escape the din of his time. It determines the tempo of his stride, slows it down or gives it wings.

Frankfurter Zeitung, February 21, 1926

24

Letter from Paris

Dear Friend,

At last spring has come to France, and our meteorological soothsayer, the Abbé Gabriel, is said to have predicted fine weather for Easter. Come and visit, there are plenty of things we can do! We can take the boat to Sèvres, past the irrigated fields of Asnières, and Sèvres-Ville d'Avray, where Gambetta died and Balzac lived. We can visit the grand, famous, and already verdant park at Saint-Cloud—more of an aristocratic wood, really—stand on the plateau from which one can overlook the whole of Paris, the cheerful wriggling of its chimneys, and the stately, dignified, and happy dance of its towers. Would you like to go to Versailles, Malmaison, Saint-Germain? Would you like to see the old cathedral of Saint-Denis? Wherever you go you will find the earth drenched with history, a cultivated nature that, with proud grace, has yielded to human wishes; humane landscapes, endowed with common sense; paths that seem to know themselves where they are going; hills that seem to know their own height; valleys that can dally with you.

There will be many people too. Buses take inquisitive Englishmen all around the outskirts of Paris, travelers of the kind we are familiar with, who need to feel they have understood something to enjoy it, and can't in any case enjoy it without taking a photograph of it. It might be an idea, therefore, to head out to Normandy, by way of Rouen. It's really not far! If we're at the Saint-Lazare Station at ten o'clock on Good Friday morning, we can lunch in Rouen at noon, with a view of the cathedral, the lean, singing central tower of Rouen Cathedral, the medieval city, whose bells are very powerful and very distant, and whose streets and lanes are of a bright and cheerful narrowness, of the sort one only finds in French towns.

And two hours after that we'd find ourselves in Le Havre, the second biggest port in France. We'd tour the old harbor together, where the little bars are: where the carousels turn and the dance halls are packed and where you can win—or lose—a lot of money. Then we can go on a walking tour of Normandy. People will stop and stare. Because in this country no one goes anywhere on foot, even though the roads are as fine and smooth as parquet floors. The livestock will be grazing in the fields. Every hour, we will hear the chimes of Lisieux, Honfleur, and Pont-l'Évêque. By night the searchlights of Le Havre stroke the dark countryside like silver hands. And always, the song of the sea.

I think we'll go to Deauville, the very ritzy, still empty, and in any case boring spa town. From there there's a direct express to Paris. Four hours.

There, doesn't that sound good to you? Come, and come soon!
Frankfurter Zeitung, April 4, 1926

25

Report from a Parisian Paradise

Paradise is downstairs, in a basement. But it's so well appointed that it almost corresponds to my notion of a seventh heaven. It's a subterranean paradise. But the direction you have to go to get there really doesn't matter. I sometimes have the feeling that if I stumble gracefully, I'll fall up in a bold flight. . . .

Blue letters light the entrance to Paradise, put together from little electric bulbs. Their blue is close to violet. It's the blue of blue pansies, and of the first morning mist to wreathe itself over a plowed field. It's the blue of vivid dreams and of cigarette smoke. It's not the blue of heaven or of the Mediterranean. You see how hard it is to describe a color.

On either side of the staircase that leads down to Paradise— paved with smooth sins but fortunately accompanied by a handrail too—are mirrored walls, which give back a different, slightly brighter blue. An atmosphere is evoked of smoke, early morning, and dreams. A very strange color is suggested, quite different from what has gone before. As a result one loses all consciousness of time. One merely remembers that it was midnight when the doors to Paradise were opened, and one went down to one's damnation. One loses one's bearings as well: all the Montmartre sky with its colorful suns of advertising, the terrestrial honking of terrestrial car horns in the rue Pigalle. One's brain has turned a misty blue. Time doesn't trickle, it surges and billows. . . .

The band sits facing the steps. There is a piano, violin, saxophone, flute, accordion, and drum. The violinist has almost nothing to do. Therefore he is the bandleader. He stands a little in front of the band, but with his back to it, facing the new arrival, the staircase, the public. He doesn't direct the music, but the room, the color, the dance. He directs Paradise. Sometimes he sings a little. He has borrowed a voice from the saxophone. He has a broad, whited-up face. He throws his arms and legs around, causing intoxication to flow from his sobriety. Because he is very sober. He is the only one here who keeps track of the time and the geographical location. He is a terrestrial, rationalist bandleader. He spends his days in bed with a newspaper. He doesn't belong to Paradise in the way that, say, I do. He is a contract worker here.

But me, I'm drinking Calvados.

Calvados is a brandy distilled from apple juice, and depending on how old it is, it can be golden brown as autumn leaves or soft yellow like amber. Sometimes it tastes like cognac and sometimes like the blossoms of otherworldly fruits. In Paradise they charge five francs a glass for it.

Tables and chairs are pushed right back, in two long rows, leaving a space for people to dance. I like to sit at the very edge. Then sometimes an angel will come by and stroke my hair. Because of course there are angels in Paradise, of course.

All races on earth are represented—white, yellow, black, brown, shaded, mixed, nuanced—with dark eyes and with light eyes, with plump lips and thin lips, bosomy and boyish, wide-hipped and slim-hipped, with knees of cool silk, they are painted brown and powdered white—in a word, they are angels.

No one knows where they come from, but they come to dance. They let men put their arms around them who really don't know the first thing about angels. They accept a lemonade when they ought to be drinking champagne. They earn very little money, and yet they give up their nights.

I'm afraid I begrudge them to some of their partners.

I begrudge them to the traveling salesmen with their padded shoulders, the salesmen who put down their case of samples somewhere and take a little peek at Paradise, and who are still utterly unmistakable. I begrudge them to the adhesive necktie sellers, floppy and invertebrate, so that you could tie them in a fashionable Windsor knot. I begrudge them to the married men from Boston, Liverpool, Amsterdam, who, briefly unsupervised, take the opportunity to press a female—an angelic—bosom to a lustful wallet.

I don't begrudge them to the sailors, those boys who never grow up, with their rolling gait, their blue eyes, and their childish collars riffled by a permanent sea wind, even here in Paradise; or to Negroes, or half-breeds, Javanese cooks, boys from Mongolia, Abyssinian princes, and heavy laborers from the markets of Paris. All of them come to Paradise. They come from the colonies, they come from the wars, they come from Tunisia, Algeria, Morocco, from the ports of Marseilles, Bordeaux, Le Havre. . . .

Sometimes Paradise feels like the great belly of a ship. The entire room is swaying gently and incessantly, and the band is chugging along. The feeling of being at once secure and lost is enough to keep me here forever. Never will it be day again, never will terrestrial reality come back, stamped by sun, work, lunch break, bells. This cellar is sailing with me over the oceans. If there's ever a moment's pause in the incessant music, it's like the endless silent moment in a storm, jammed in between lightning and thunder, fearful, breathless, with no heartbeat.

All at once the illumination changes. It switches to the profound blue-green of meadows at night, then to a dark ruby red. Lips turn blue, and the cigarette in my hand is a little stick with a silvery glow, and attached to it is a fine mesh of woven ash. Then Paradise turns orange-yellow. The unaccompanied accordion plays a song, with human sighs as it draws breath, a song that's situated somewhere between Europe and Africa, like a little island, an orange-yellow melody. It has something unspecifiably folkloric about it, it could be from anywhere, it reminds me of Slavic summer nights. It's as though the accordion were producing the golden yellow light. It's an evening instrument. It produces and sustains this exaggerated sunset, without sun: the end of the world.

Everyone knows they are lost. The girls become more lost than ever. Even the traveling salesmen would like to cry.

But they mustn't, and they don't. With its dying sigh the accordion extinguishes the orange light, and the flute rekindles the silver on the ceiling.

New arrivals, sentenced to Paradise, are sent our way by the street. A new angel arrives: pale yellow, octoroon; in her delicate face a broad, always-open mouth. It shows a set of strong white teeth, a gentle menace.

It is one of the unfathomable mysteries of nature, why this woman with her big strong teeth should have such humble, fragile ankles; why her feet don't tread on the steps so much as kiss them.

Frankfurter Zeitung, April 14, 1926

26

Saint-Quentin, Péronne, Maisonnette

Omnibuses are still going out to the battlefields, large, comfortable, well-sprung omnibuses. The Thomas Cook Company is at pains to keep any physical shocks away from its clients. It is interested only in emotional shocks. The visit costs 120 francs per person per day. Eight years of peace have already passed over the fields of honor; the world war is a little worn now, but 120 francs per day is a tempting offer. Large, comfortable, well-sprung omnibuses are driving out to the battlefields.

I don't take advantage of Thomas Cook's offer. I go by train to Saint-Quentin. I get on the train that goes from Paris via Berlin to Warsaw, which has only first- and second-class carriages. The passengers are just betaking themselves to their wagons-lit as they pass the battlefields. A few are unable to sleep. Is it the memories? Is it their consciences? Oh, it's probably only the uncomfortable beds. The unaccustomed jolting of the wheels. Do they even know they are passing the battlefields? No one looks out the window at Saint-Quentin. The train sets down a small scattering of passengers and a large bundle of mail on the benighted platform. Then it's on its way to Berlin and Warsaw.

The streets of the town of Saint-Quentin are lit by the moon and a couple of helpful streetlights. The weather is cool, spring is not quite here yet, the clouds have silver edges, and rain is forecast for tomorrow. The road that leads from the station to the town goes gently downhill and twists a little. It's a sad road. There are no trees lining it. There are boxy houses like wardrobes, with drawers for people to creep into. And it smells of war. That smell again, eight years after the great conflagration, the smell of old fire and mortar dust, a bittersweet putrescence that always wafted out to greet us when we took up position in a town that had been shelled. Smells live longer than events, and longer than memories. The pestilential stink of a shell outlives the devastation it wreaks. Life is noisier than death, and the eye sometimes can't see a grave for flowers. But the nose still sniffs out ancient devastations; of all the sense organs, it has the longest memory. I can smell I'm in a war zone even before I set foot in it.

And now visible memories fall in. Either side of the road there are dead houses of the familiar type, and sudden, ugly, burnished, new houses, with a proliferation of signs. They stand all alone; they won't have neighbors for a year or two; they aren't based on anything; they are no continuation of anything; they aren't even a beginning, they are purely provisional. Between a building site, with piles of bricks and planks, and a brown wall with blind window holes through which you see the sky, there is one of these tall, white, narrow houses, like a solitary, exaggeratedly white tooth. This town could be somewhere in the American Wild West. It was an old European town, with an old European history. Shells wiped it out.

There was once a house here, or a warehouse, or a factory. Now, there is just a thirty-foot length of wall, roughly six-feet-tall, its edges jagged, as though gnawed by some unearthly breed of super rodent. Next to this length of wall lie a few piles of bricks that once made up the rest of the house. Behind it, there's a dusty, gray piece of uneven wasteland, with a tiny little tump in the middle. On it there's a single luminous yellow wildflower. What a tiny dead-light for such a big, strong corpse!

There's a dumb, cheerless piece of masonry in the background. Here you can read the past: clear evidence of rooms, passages, doorways. The limestone has loyally preserved them: squares, right angles, straight edges. They are like the traces of large symmetrical nests that had once been stuck to the wall. I visualize how the nests came down one day, and the fledglings lay there with broken necks.

Here is a defunct well that will never give water again, with a stiffly extended pump handle sticking out like a withered arm. Here is an inextricably tangled knot of barbed wire on a wooden post, a weed of human sowing, a mixture of thorns, creepers, dried vegetables, and tin wreaths. Here are round huts, roofed with corrugated iron, and economical little square windows. They look oddly romantic, like tents for traveling circus people. But they are apartments where solid people, established inhabitants of Saint-Quentin, must live. They live as if in tanks. Old war matériel has given them a roof. When the rain falls on it, it must sound like the old familiar bombardment that not long ago they would have heard all round them.

The town is large and dark, and fast asleep. It's only partly a town. Every few steps it's reduced—to a village, a camp, a campsite. Cafés and bars are accommodated in huts, like little sutlers' or camp followers' businesses. The marketplace is bleak, and my shadow lies stretched out for a long time on its uneven cobbles. Golden light spills out of the one remaining café. It's high-ceilinged, illuminated, and empty. Its revolving door doesn't move. Its four glass wings are as stiff as the wings of a vertically pinned butterfly. The waiters are reading the paper, and the barmaid is sitting like a sentry in a bombproof shelter, with bottles all around her.

The saddest place of all is the square under my hotel window. It's a meaningless little square that owes its existence to the circumstance that the road bends at that point. Subsequently, to comfort it, a little water basin and fountain—emblem of everlasting mirth—were installed there. The fountain, though, doesn't have enough pressure; it won't spurt into the air properly; it's botched, dwarfish, a runt of a water jet; it falls back quickly, and makes more noise and a heavier splash than it should. That noise is the only thing I can hear. That and, from the station, the forever-yearning whistles of locomotives.

IN THE MORNING, as promised, it rains.

I want to drive from Saint-Quentin to Péronne, the site of the great battle of the Somme. The road is good, wide and inviting. In spite of the rain, I'm going to get out at Bovincourt and walk the rest of the way. I must. Does one drive from one grave to the next? Does one drive through cemeteries?

Because these *are* cemeteries, even where there are no crosses to be seen. The soil is nourished by corpses. It's still ripped and scored, covered with thick lesions, from which a thin covering of grass has begun to sprout, like a growth of beard on a ravaged face. The trenches are slowly beginning to heal over. Gradually rusted shells decay. But deep in the ground there are still unexploded projectiles. Sometimes they come to the surface. By the side of the road there are bits of metal equipment, bowls, buckets, bullets and fragments of bullets. The scorched trees are stuck with shrapnel.

There are no more horrifying monuments than these trees— these black, riven stumps, scorched at the top, with their roots still in the ground but now devoid of function, rotting and splintering, each one a devastated world, each stump a kind of inverse tree, each one its own gallows tree, riddled or studded with bullets, each one with rags of bark hanging off it, home for insects and lead, still smelling of fire and gas. These stumps are the particular crop that has taken here.

Some, already, are going green. Way down, just above the roots, there are little green shoots, new leaves and flowers. They are already getting into their peacetime uniform! Already they have forgotten! What a powerful thing life is!

Here is the cemetery full of iron crosses, not the ones that are pinned on chests, but the real ones that stand over burial mounds. This is the German cemetery at Bovincourt, the final resting place of forty thousand unidentified soldiers. Veterans are forever coming to look for missing comrades. The French warden goes around, makes a point of shaking hands with every German he meets, and asks: "Comrade, what was it all for?" The inevitable question of all those tending war cemeteries. The presence of forty thousand unidentified dead soldiers inclines one toward pacifism.

The old cathedral at Péronne has been shot to pieces. Gray planks have been nailed up where its gates once were. Stone statues of saints, once sheltered in portals and niches and corners, are now exposed to the elements. The church has no roof and a hundred shell holes. It should have been left to stand, the old cathedral, as a kind of twofold monument. But because life is stronger, people lose their respect and their awe, and they push up against the ruins of the church, which, even in destruction, are still imposing; raw red-brick houses press the ruins into service to prop them up. People are building all over Péronne. Scaffolding climbs nimbly and lithely into the air. The new town hall is already finished. Men are working on every street. Yes, even notorious Maisonnette, the most terrible battlefield on the Somme, is covered with fresh green and new seed and thick new underbrush. The earth here was turned over, spattered with chunks of limestone, and with mud that oozed up from the depths. There wasn't a blade of grass or vegetation. Millions of shells rained down. A division clung for months to the tiny hillside. It was a division in hell. And in the distance they saw the silver water of the Somme, and behind it the shining red roofs of Péronne, and on the left the green, blooming land—the other country, enemy country, that they yearned for as for a woman.

Now larks fizz through the air; the rain has stopped; the wind has blown away the clouds. Anyone who didn't see the war would think this was peace. But I can sense red blood running through the veins of the surviving trees, through the clumps of earth, in the delicate filaments of leaves. The spring smells of powder and shot. Swallows are errant projectiles. The sky presses down. It bears not clouds but destruction. The wind scatters billions of tiny pieces of shrapnel. Trees groan like dying men. Twigs snap like rifle locks. Bent over the landscape, like a general over a map, is God. Unapproachable as a general; remote as a general. . . .

Frankfurter Zeitung, May 2, 1926

27

The Troubadour

This was exactly how I'd pictured the "victor" who doesn't despise the pen, although his first love is of course the sword. Once installed in his quarters in enemy country, he unbuckles the latter and picks up the former (whips it out, he might say), and starts rifling through drawers for erotic perquisites. His chosen field is what the enemy reads to get in the mood.

In his idle hours he records what goes through what passes for his mind. In the officers' mess he has a reputation for bookishness, and for being something of an egghead. He's the type of fellow of whom his comrades would say: "Major Delmar? You'd like him! Scribbles a bit on the side!"

Perhaps he composes occasional odes for regimental celebrations too. A bit of an all-rounder. File between Apollo and Mars. And what does he mostly scribble? Diaries, memoirs, and so-called *aperçus*.

A protracted campaign in France, of the type that the Almighty laid on for us between '14 and '18, is enough to get a whole book out of the major. He wrote it in his idle moments, I can see him parking his charger and getting on to his trusty Pegasus. The book is called *French Women: Experiences, Observations, Musings, Paradoxes*.

The author is Maximilian Delmar; Ernst Günther in Freiburg is the publisher.

I quote:

"Eros is a jester, who plays his games until the catastrophe is at hand. The essence of a woman's love is play. I therefore declare the joke to be the apt vehicle for this treatise."

So there we are. The worst thing that could happen to me in life is a messroom wag. The consequences of his antic disposition are indescribable and can only be quoted:

"[In France] we are confronted with territory where neither Danish frigidity obtains, nor yet the torrid passion of nights in Naples or Seville.

"Climatologically, the spring months, generally the most favorable for human passion, offer the pleasant alternation between warm days and cool nights, so beloved of all ardent women.

"The Frenchwoman will only believe in a man's maturity once he has successfully passed her test. She measures a man's intellect by the organ that chiefly pays homage to her.

"The further tale of Fifi's wedding night passed off in the darkness and silence of a Nice hotel room."

Once the major has delivered himself of a couple of pages on sex in the cities, he ends so:

"With these few words, I have said all I have to say on the subject of sex in the city." (Full stop. The end. No whispering at the back.)

"The French virgin is out for a husband for herself, and not a lover." (No luck, then, it would appear, for the major.)

"Her wedding day determines the future course of every Frenchwoman's life.

"No man who has not kissed such tears knows anything about

the pleasure an adulterous Frenchwoman is capable of bestowing."
(So he did get lucky after all.)

He has been gathering experience, the major, no doubt about
it! He's read his Balzac, his Goncourt brothers, his Flaubert, his
Maupassant, and padded out his work with sizable chunks of the
classics. He is a master of pornographic suggestion. No garter, no
comb, no bedside drawer, no postcard—nothing in his enemy bil-
let is safe from his wanton interpretation. He's not so different,
the major, from schoolboys underlining words like desire, bodice,
bosom, and going straight to the bit of the Ten Commandments
about coveting thy neighbor's wife.

All this would be a private matter of no concern to us were it
not that the major has gone public: a man of honor, pulling back
curtains, nosing around in bedrooms, revealing secrets that give
himself away. He is long since stripped to the skin, he stands there
naked before us. This too mightn't be too disagreeable. But he has
forgotten to unbuckle his saber, and its rattle is off-putting. You
see his major's stripes even on his nightshirt.

Here is a man whom one would prefer to pass over in silence,
were it not that he has had the impudence, following the lost war
of all lost wars, to go back to a country whose cemeteries are full
to bursting, to assemble his memories of night tables and his messroom anecdotes. He was not one who remained behind on the
great graveyard that for him would be a field of honor. But instead
of thanking his Creator for the undeserved favor, he goes out with
a smirk on his face and tells everyone he's been to a boudoir.

And nothing stirs. No hand is raised, no invalid puts out his
crutches. The dead are as silent as women in adultery.

Frankfurter Zeitung, May 9, 1926

28

La Renaissance Latine

I had no business in the "Grande Salle des Societés Savantes"; it was pure chance that brought me there. Professor Achille Mestre of the Institut Catholique, the Abbé Yves de la Brière, and several other figures were seated on the podium. The auditorium was jam-packed with students, sitting and standing. The chairman was Henri Massis, editor in chief of the *Revue Universelle*, which is the publication of the Latin renaissance. From the speeches I heard, but also from printed announcements, I was given to understand that the aim of the "Renaissance latine" is to counter the "ill effects of Teutonic and Bolshevik culture."

How do you go about doing something like that? Well, you gather together students from every Latin country, students, therefore, from Belgium, Canada, Spain, Italy, Portugal, the French-speaking part of Switzerland and the French-speaking Middle East, throw in a few Mexicans, Argentines, Brazilians, if available, nor do you turn your nose up at the Romanians, of whom there are a great number at Parisian universities—even though they are certainly not of pure Latin blood, or Latin culture either. And then you tell them that they are all more or less descended from Rome, giving them a direct line to Julius Caesar and to Roman law, to Horace and the Pope, to Latin logic, and to the Catholic Church.

When they heard this, the assembled fascists in the hall went delirious. They had come with photographs—as if one wouldn't recognize them otherwise—of Mussolini, cheap, mass-produced prints of the heroic Mussolini, raising the palm of his hand in the face of the onlooker, as if to brook no contradiction. This, the reader may know, is the fascist salute.

Those students who are equipped with this photograph now begin to sing—I imagine it's probably the fascist hymn, I'm not familiar with it. Singing like that, they look quite indistinguishable from the German swastika brigades. It would appear that national anthems, whose purpose is to stoke national feeling against other nations, may have quite the opposite effect: namely to make all peoples, or their singing parts at least, one.

Professor Achille Mestre said Rome had brought logic and order, organization and authority, to the world. Well, really! And there I was thinking "organization" was a thoroughly German affair, a German invention, even! The Middle Ages, the professor says, were a shining period, an example of a time when "authority" prevailed. Freedom, says the professor, is unnecessary. We can see peoples dissatisfied with their "freedom" now requesting "a strong hand," if not "an iron fist." Revolution was a calamity! There was nothing we needed as much as "authority."

"Catholicism"—the speakers all agreed on this—was a specifically Latin affair too. The Catholic Church was a guarantor of Latin culture, and it was the Latin peoples who supported the Catholic Church. And there sat the Abbé de la Brière and applauded. He applauded speakers who relegated the Catholic Church to a tribal church. He himself went on to speak about the Poles, a "Slavic people that, though wedged between Bolshevism and the Germans, had managed to protect Latin civilization, and whose outstanding representatives had successfully mastered the Latin language."

It is not to be assumed that Professor de la Brière, a teacher at the Institut Catholique, a distinguished French man of letters, and an extremely polished speaker, is *un*aware that outstanding representatives of the Germans, the British, the Scandinavians—the "Germanic" peoples, then—or the Russians—the "Bolshevists"— do not also have Latin civilization, and that the Germans in particular probably boast at least as many experts on Roman law and on Horace, Tacitus, and Julius Caesar as do the French and Italians. I do not assume that de la Brière, the trusty servant of the Catholic Church, is out to restrict the influence of his church to the so-called Latin peoples. Monsieur de la Brière is well aware that we are all heirs to Rome, and he knows that, for example, the Germans have inherited more Latin culture than—once again, for example—the Romanians.

So why does he applaud? Why do Latin renaissances begin with singing fascists? Where is the axis between the Portuguese and the Romanian Slavs? Is there not a much stronger axis between the French of Latin culture and the Germans of Latin culture?

Isn't a new *Europe* a healthier idea than this "Renaissance latine"?

Why? Why?

Frankfurter Zeitung, May 15, 1926

29

Twenty Minutes from Before the War

In a Parisian cinema they are showing old newsreel footage—infinitely past, because sundered from us by the war—of such dusty novelties as the fashions, the dances, the five-o'clock teas, of an era that waltzed straight out of its pathetic whimsicality into a bloody horror: an epoch so deceitful that it didn't even experience the truth of its own demise. It was already dead by the time it died. Its children were living ghosts, having been molded from papiermâché in, oh, let's say, pergolas.

These old films, changed every time there's a change of program, appear under the heading *"Twenty Minutes from Before the War."* It's because of them that the cinema is sold out every day, and sometimes full to bursting. The sons all want to go, to laugh at their fathers. The great family album of the past is opened up before their eyes. It is made up of graves that elicit not shudders of horror but irresistible mirth. The effect of the pictures is like that of twenty top hats at a funeral: The hats are so ridiculous that they rather take the edge off the coffin. The result is a rather peculiar sort of dread that touches not the soul but the funny bone.

We are parked in front of the screen, watching one of those old Prussian army parades: the regiments goose-stepping by in honor of the kaiser; the horses' tails flicking and tossing—some where nature put them, other for some reason attached to helmets; the feisty earnest faces, squeezed out of stiff collars and given a false double chin, lackeys in frock coats, beards of yellow thread. Sweat keeps dripping—eagerly, proudly, sweatily—onto starch-creaking shirtfronts, gleaming cuffs of some canvaslike tin keep slipping over hands busy throwing off hats, waving flags. We see the Parisian crowds of 1910, turned out to see the French president, men carrying rolled-up sausages of black silk (which are umbrellas in a state of repose), with pince-nez on broad ribbons that sway in the breeze like hammocks for flies, with cravats spilling across chests like floppy mattresses on bedframes. We see women with long trains that look like carpets that have accidentally gotten caught under their feet, in wraps that suddenly and dramatically bell out at the hips, in little bonnets of all kinds teetering on top of vast, unsteady towers of hair, and therefore held in place with kitchen skewers. The women all look like round towers, wide at the bottom, narrower further up; when they stand up, their dresses hide their feet, actually the dresses are fixed to the sidewalk by means of a wire grid. At the very top of the tower are three gibbering glass cherries.

We see the very latest Parisian dance sensation of 1908, demonstrated for us by the most famous professor *de danse* of the period. He wears a set of tails and white waistcoat, a stiff collar around his neck like a smooth fortification, a small, curled, black moustache. He has tiny little feet, and he dances on tiptoe; between thumb and middle finger he holds the thumb and middle finger of his partner. He sashays two steps forward, one step back, spins around, lays his head coquettishly on his shoulder, sees what his little feet are doing, and cleverly bats his eyelids in time to his movements.

We see the latest creations of one great old fashion house: From neck to hips the models are paneled in satin, from their hips down to the fake Persian rug, they are curtains from provincial stages. Sometimes things get wildly indecent and they expose an elbow, scandalous creatures! And when they sit down, they pluck up a skirt with two fingers, flash us an ankle, and we die. Oh, the suggestive panderings of fashion! Large wire-mesh dinner plates covered with velvet and tulle wobble on heads, peacocks' tails sway on the plates, fall into faces like fly whisks. Draped over the front of the dresses are these bedside rugs, triangular, ending in a tassel. All the women, when they smile, lay their heads on one shoulder. And when are they ever not smiling, the flirts? They bat their eyelids open and shut like precious cabinets, full of promises.

We see prewar feature films, for instance the one about the forger. The young man passes false bills so as to be able to afford the requirements of his wicked, immoral, and buttoned-up-to-the-chin beloved. He is apprehended; his mother comes; he stands hidden behind a screen. He plunges forth, the moral fervor of his remorse causes the screen to fall, he follows suit, prostrates himself on the floor, gets up, hoisted by a divine, invisible string, then, with extended, leverlike arms, flings himself round his mother's feather boa.

These are the sort of shocking displays we now put ourselves through, we, the children of the present day, we, who have gotten over Darwin and Ibsen, give ourselves over to the exotic woman with the "*pleureuse*" veil, the suffragette, the parade uniform, the umbrella, the large man with the goatee, the train, and the towering hairdo made of pigtails and spikes; we, who go to Negro revues and watch naked girls, we toughened and bred in drum fire, scornful of beautiful lies, we devotees, as we would have it, of the ugly truth. We sit in front of the whole deceitful misery of our fathers, who appear to have invented the cinema purely to show us themselves in their full absurdity, and we laugh, we laugh. We have prizefighters and sports fans, America and endurance runners, girls drilled by preachers, a whole internationale of Sunday windbreakers. But we don't have bodices instead of breasts, feather boas instead of necks, curtains instead of legs, and top hats in place of mourning! Where the goose-step is still practised, we *know* it's dead; really, at the worst, the parades of our time are to celebrate living memorials (not dead ones). We know that once we had the "*pleureuse*," the steel helmet was only a matter of time, that there's a straight path from the modest veil to the gas mask, and from the pergola to the trench. And those unarmed reservists who plowed the fields of honor and sowed us there with their pathetic blessings—that deceitful eve of the war is something that makes us laugh our heads off every evening, for twenty minutes, and no longer.

Frankfurter Zeitung, June 11, 1926

30

Books About Soldiers

France—Czechoslovakia—Germany

Joseph Delteil, the famous author of *Jeanne d'Arc*, has set himself to write an epic on the Great War; to sing a hymn to *Les Poilus*—as his book, published by Édition du Loup (Paris), is called; to treat not the historical facts but the aura of those facts; not the letter but the spirit. Delteil's aim is to detach the human story from the awe and the historical pageant, the personal (both tragic and beautiful) from the monumental—he wants to portray not the soldier but, as he says, the *poilu*.

This book, which caused a sensation when it appeared in France, could only have been written in France. It remains, I think, a well-intentioned effort. Historical proximity inevitably gets in the way of epic objectivity. But even from greater chronological distance, the '14–'18 war will never make a Trojan War; and even if Delteil were Homer, he couldn't write an Iliad about the siege of Paris. A war that has been so comprehensively gotten over and seen through, whose measureless tragedy grew out of such petty quibbles among emperors and diplomats, cannot (even in France) be treated with epic bravura but cries out for satire. Delteil has written (whatever he may think) with subjectivity; his book is a lyrical document that traces the atmospheric shifts of our "great epoch."

The grisly truth of the "great epoch" can only be encompassed by caricature. The Czech writer Jaroslav Hašek has portrayed it. His book is entitled *The Adventures of the Good Soldier Schweik During the World War*.

THE GOOD SOLDIER Schweik is a little Czech dog seller, a simpleton, utterly clueless about the big things of the world, and still, in all his helplessness, able to deal with them. The fool Schweik reveals the heroic age as a gruesome accumulation of stupidity that can't even deal with him—not even *him*. Faced with the healthy horse sense of this notorious imbecile, the whole edifice that historians, scholars, politicians, emperors, kings, presidents, industrialists, and poets have worked to build has no chance.

They say of God that he likes to speak through the mouths of fools. In Jaroslav Hašek's book he even speaks through the mouth of a man released from the military on account of his medically confirmed imbecility. The idiot is even better at unmasking lies and pathos than is the satirist. The good soldier Schweik is so foolish as to be wise. There is something still more foolish than folly, which is stupidity. The world war was an instance of such. And Schweik proves it.

Hašek's book was assembled from pieces that the author wrote during the war in Russia for a daily column in a newspaper for Czech legionnaires. He subsequently became a Communist. Had he not died so young, who knows, he might have written another book in which his new Czech fatherland was ironized like his previous Austrian one. He was not able to revise this book about Schweik before it was published.

It does have occasional longueurs, and could do with being edited. Nor is the German translation what it ought to be. I seem to remember once reading a couple of chapters from it in a German periodical, in a dazzling translation. What happened to that? It's so difficult, putting this outskirts-of-Prague dog seller's dialect into German, the publisher should really have taken the trouble to find a distinguished translator, someone who knows Prague, and who knows German.

HAŠEK GIVES US the witty caricature of a soldier. The late Philipp Mainländer, a respectable, estimable, though not especially original philosopher (died by his own hand, in 1876), gives us the unwitting caricature. Walter Rauschenberger has done a disservice to the memory of the good philosopher by publishing the manuscript of his memoir: *My Life as a Soldier*. I could have wished the late Mainländer had found a more discriminating literary executor and a better literary stylist. When Rauschenberger writes in his introduction: "Anthropologically speaking, it should be pointed out that Mainländer was of average height and dark-haired"—then I can already guess what, militarily speaking, Mainländer himself will have to say on the subject. And it was certainly news to me that the poor man had been turned down for the army in 1866. "In autumn 1868," writes Mainländer, "I was utterly at liberty, and my first thought of course was to join the army, so that I could be present at the beginning of any further war." He doesn't succeed, I'm afraid.

Finally (albeit only *after* the Franco-Prussian War of 1870–71), the philosopher does get to be a soldier. Before he gets his marching orders, he prepares himself as follows:

Every day I set aside half an hour to prepare myself for my new profession. I did a "slow march" (the blue harebells and yellow broom tittered to themselves, and the fat bumblebees mocked me), and I practiced bayonet drill: right thrust! Left thrust! Jab! The interplay of these two diametrically opposed activities— pure sensibility on the one hand and pure irritability on the other—left me in a somewhat peculiar condition.

Poor old Mainländer! He is nearsighted—zealous, zestful, enthusiastic, but nearsighted. And so, the day before the official examination he presents himself nervously to the rather perplexed surgeon major, is promised that, come what may, he will get to be a soldier, and so he does.

He becomes a soldier, and naively, childishly, sentimentally, he describes army life. And Rauschenberger edits it. And so exposes Mainländer, who might have occupied a good, quiet entry in some dictionary of philosophy as a "three-year volunteer." And a publisher publishes it. And a paper mill supplies the paper. And typesetters set it. And booksellers sell it. And I—I review it.

I review it as a tiny, an infinitesimal, indication of the way things are in Germany.

Frankfurter Zeitung, August 15, 1926

31

A Day or Two in Deauville

I love the Gare Saint-Lazare and the trains that leave from there. It's a lively station, with lots of unnecessary shops selling lots of unnecessary things that are meant to be indispensable for travelers: for instance, easily breakable bottles and mirrors, heavy leather cases for manicure items that would be better off in your sponge bag, patented inkwell carriers that you have to hold in your hand in case they open. And who are these annoying little things for? For rich people. And where do rich people travel? If it's the "season," they're off to Deauville.

Yes, it's the season in Deauville. Even now special steamers are leaving New York for Le Havre/Deauville; the crossing takes six days, a mere hop across the pond. You can leave London at nine o'clock at night, and be in Deauville at seven the following morning. And from Paris (lucky Paris!) the journey is only three hours—Deauville is just 184 kilometers away.

The train I board offers only first- and second-class accommodation, and is quite determined not to make any stops on the way. It's a haughty train; it seems to me it must despise the country it passes through. With scathing rattle, it speeds through any stations that happen not to be fashionable spa towns, and practically ignores the salutes of the unfortunate stationmasters. We are rich people, we passengers. We mustn't get bored on the train; we want to get bored on the beach. If it did occur to the train to stop somewhere en route, why, then we could afford to get off and climb on an airplane. We have our destination, and we want to get there—and we don't want to stop anywhere else on the way. We are sitting in large, bright, spacious carriages; we can open and close the windows easily with just two fingers (when does that ever happen?); the doors close by themselves so that none of us can fall out, even if he breaks the rules and leans against them; there are no third-class passengers here to bother us—none of those people who get on in towns that don't have "seasons"—none of those people who even in the period between the Grand Prix and the first fashion show of the autumn pursue their disgusting little occupations—we are, as they say, *entre nous*.

We are *entre nous*, which is to say there aren't any sick people among us either, we're just fashionable. Doctors sometimes recommend Deauville, they even prescribe it, but only to healthy patients. Deauville is the typical fashionable sea-bathing spot. It consists of a beach, a horizon, clean, white, silent houses, a noisy casino, sports lawns, a racetrack, café terraces, restaurants. It's not a natural product, even though all the amenities that nature can produce have been carefully and selectively included. Inasmuch as nature is prepared to bestow something of its riches on the upper crust of society, and inasmuch as these find it compatible with their dignity to accept such gifts, gratis—only in that way is Deauville natural. In general appearance it looks as though it has been drawn up by an architect who specializes in sanatoriums. Its sports lawns are of a double and triple greenness, its waves crash in with triple strength. If I see a gardener watering the flowers in Deauville, I very much doubt that it's water he has in his can; I would suspect perfume instead, garden perfume by Houbigant.* Here, roses, violets, and pansies grow in private gardens, fashion salon creations, artificial flowers that the beautiful women of the world—those women that never fade—attach to their fashionable gowns.

Of course, one doesn't arrive in Deauville itself—come, come! One arrives in Trouville, its less favored sister town, which has agreed to house a railway station. Because even the presence of a station is unhealthy. A station spreads coal fumes, and in Deauville they don't want any sort of fumes like that. Trouville is a dear old Norman town with gabled houses, with shops, with cars and cabs. Without Trouville, Deauville couldn't be Deauville. Trouville supplies Deauville with the humdrum necessities of life.

Admittedly Trouville has its own hotels and its own beach. But they are bourgeois hotels and a bourgeois beach. Outsiders like me stay in Trouville and swim in Trouville. During the season, even so, we spend thirty to fifty francs a day for a room. If we had the courage—which costs money too—to move to Deauville, then we'd be spending two hundred francs for a room.

But we don't have the courage or we don't have the money. (It's hard to say where cowardice ends and impecuniousness begins.) As far as I'm concerned, even I am confused. I wander over to Deauville in the afternoon only in performance of my duties. I think of myself as rich. In a gentleman's fashion magazine I read an article called: *"Conseils à Jean Jacques avant son départ pour Deauville."* Ooh, such advice! "My dear friend," thus the counselor,

> I picture you getting out of bed the morning after your arrival, wearing pajamas with a sober pattern, somewhat at variance

---

*The House of Houbigant's most popular fragrance (for decades) was Quelques Fleurs.

with your character; but in a color that accords with it—bright, then, for all the gravity, though of course not loud. They are some of those English crêpe de chine pajamas that are so pleasant to wear. A knock on your door! You call out: Enter! And with all the alacrity of youth, you leap out of your pajamas into a breakfast suit of a young and lively color, very soft and delicate, a pleasant contrast to your pajamas, though, like them, also of crêpe de chine, and edged with a discreet pattern. You smoke a couple of cigarettes to dispel the boredom of waiting for your morning swim. Once bathed, you look for an appropriate morning outfit in your suitcase. And there—what is it you find?—a pair of white buckskin shoes, with yellow kid trim—yellow, mind, not red!—with no pattern, no holes, no buckles, such soft shoes, but with stout soles, a perfect team with your yellow jacket and your white trousers with the intermittent blue stripe.

Oh dear, and there I am in a dark gray summer suit. My heart is also heavy, I must confess, because when I heard a knock on my door, I stayed in my pajamas, not leaping into a morning suit, and because said pajamas were white with navy stripes. Also, my shoes are not white buckskin but perfectly ordinary, even rather offensive, yellow kid. Will they even let me into the casino?

I *am* allowed to pass into the casino—where they play roulette (in the larger room) and baccarat (in the smaller). Only men are admitted. A year ago the Parisian actress Yvonne Printemps bet that she would be allowed in. She got in, and won ten thousand dollars. She had to put on men's clothing. In all probability the white buckskin shoes described above. Monsieur Citroën, the Parisian automobile king, is a regular guest at the casino. He stays in Deauville each year from July to the end of August, loses lots of money in the casino, and, rumor has it that before going back to Paris, he gives each croupier one of his automobiles as a present.

Monsieur Citroën has a villa in Deauville. It stands gleaming white, a jewel among houses, on a side street, a quiet side street, where not even a Citroën car is permitted to honk. Next to the Citroën villa is the house of Monsieur Rothschild. It's closed today, Monsieur Rothschild hasn't arrived yet from Paris, his gardener is going around with a watering can, his footman isn't wearing his livery, the horses are whinnying in their stables, the flowerbeds are waiting colorfully for Monsieur Rothschild. He is expected next week.

Villas, villas, nothing but villas! There is a boulevard, the Boulevard Eugene Corniché, where no mortal house dares to stand. All the villas have Norman facades, cosy gables, little balconies, steep roofs, vine-hung verandas. It's a style that, while not traditional, has borrowed from tradition to remind people that Deauville is in Normandy. It might occur to one of the wealthy Americans who come here to take a photograph of the Boulevard Corniché, to show the folks at home something "typically Norman." If the grandstand at Deauville has a Norman gable, with brown crossbeams, reminiscent of the delicately striped pattern on a pair of morning trousers, that "style" is nothing more than a concession on the part of the spa administration to the ethnological curiosity of the guests, who would like a little more to remember than cement bathing huts.

There are cement bathing huts in Deauville, so you don't catch cold; a boardwalk connecting the sea and the administration; café terraces where you can drink a glass of orangeade in your bathing costume, gratis, because you don't carry a wallet in the water, and so instead you are given credits; three polo fields; two hundred horses for rent; "Pompeiian baths" with classical round pools and modern Negro jazz bands; hotel lobbies where they have "*thés dansants*"; artificial moonlight for romantically inclined billionaires who don't want to be at the mercy of the weather forecast; and ebb- and floodtide regulated by the spa administration. Only once a year, on a Sunday in August, is there contact with any plebeian element: On that occasion there is a sort of Norman fancy-dress party, where everyone appears in folk costume. But then, on closer inspection, it turns out that a good many of those wearing costumes hail from New York's Park Avenue and the Champs-Élysées in Paris. They say that the sand at Deauville is sprinkled fresh every year by Coty—to publicize his purchase of *Le Figaro*.* But that's an exaggeration.

Frankfurter Zeitung, August 28, 1927

*The cosmetics magnate Francois Coty acquired his majority holding in the newspaper in 1922.

32

Emile Zola—Author Away from His Desk

Dear Gerhart Pohl,

Your kind invitation to take part in your assessment of Zola's influence on contemporary German writing has only just reached me—and a moment after I read in the newspaper that Sacco and Vanzetti have been put to death. By the time your readers get to see this, the connection between these judicial murders in America and the greatest servant of French justice will not appear quite as obvious as it does at the time of writing; it may even strike some as contrived. Permit me, though, to follow the thought that was never far from my mind as I was reading about that gruesome affair: There is no longer a Zola in the world!

I can't say whether he might have been able to prevent this murder, today (after the war) and in America (the land of unlimited inhumanity). But the fact that not one of our "world-famous" authors bestirred himself over this matter strikes me, as their contemporary, as more than merely embarrassing: It could even spell the end of such hopes as we still have. The belief that justice—here and in America—is dead must cast a chill on all our hearts. Zola, I am sure, would have had the courage to go on fighting, even in a hopeless cause. It was his conviction that the future will have its revenge on the sins of the present; and that the future belongs to the poor of today, the destitute.

Only a blind man could fail to see that even the "purely literary" effect of a writer's work is inextricably bound up with his role as a public figure and a citizen; with his deep commitment to the present day, and everything to do with it: the people, the bitterness of poverty, and the implacability of wealth and the laws governing it. No one can abstract himself from the earth on which he lives. There is no dividing line between a response to obvious public wrongdoing, and the brave pursuit of work "*sub specie aeternitatis.*" A man who is not immediately stirred to action by a newspaper report on a violation of human rights has forfeited the right to describe human actions and figures in his books. In his passionate concern for reality, Zola removed the distinction between the "profane" and the "noble." A specious distinction, set up and maintained by reactionaries, in any case. What they want is to establish a category of "icons"—to go on and sell tickets for them. Zola was the first European writer to do without a desk as an object of inspiration, the first novelist with a notebook. The first author on a locomotive.

It is as such that he can be an example to Germany, of all countries. We have authors here who are chronically deskbound. We have the fable of the blind seers, and the curse of professional aesthetes. Which prominent German author bothered himself about the Black Reichswehr,* massacred workers, Bavarian justice,†

---

*The Black Reichswehr were secret right-wing paramilitary organizations set up in violation of the Versailles treaty; they instigated a rebellion in 1923.

†"Bavarian justice" is probably a reference to Hitler's trial for treason in a Munich court (February and March 1923) after the failed Kapp putsch. The court was lenient, sentencing him to five years, of which he served just nine months (during which he wrote *Mein Kampf*).

Pomerania and the excesses of the von Kähnes? How many Dreyfus affairs have we had since 1918 alone? Which of our celebrities
have ever so much as looked at a train driver?—though they must
have written about them.

They have no right to castigate Zola for his "shallow" natural-
ism. It was the literary mode that went with a powerful belief in
the power of reality. Only by minute observation of reality do you
get at the truth.

I hope you and your readers will excuse me for these few rushed
sentences, and remain, with comradely greeting, your

Joseph Roth
Die Neue Bücherschau, 1927

33

The Living Buddha

P aul Morand,* who famously grew up as a Buddhist, has written a novel, *The Living Buddha* which has just appeared in
German translation from Insel Publishers.

Morand tells the story of the Buddhist crown prince Djali of
Karastra, who leaves his homeland in the company of a French
friend to go to Europe, gets to know it inside out, uses his visit as
an occasion to reflect on parallels between the life of Buddha and
his own, and finally, after a doomed love affair with a young American girl has failed on the usual grounds of racial prejudice, returns
home to occupy the throne of his fathers and make do with being
a king, having failed in his bid to be a white man.

So far as I'm concerned, I found more parallels between *Alt-
Heidelberg†* and this story of Morand's than between Djali and
Buddha. The hard lot of an heir to the throne who is forced to
renounce love and happiness because he has, as it were, the crown

---

*The extremely popular French author (1888–1976) was a longtime resident
of Vevey, Switzerland.

†*Alt-Heidelberg* was the title of the novel and the play by Wilhelm Meyer
Förster (1862–1934) on which Sigmund Romberg's famous operetta *The Student
Prince* was based.

of Damocles forever hanging over him, is something we in Germany are familiar with from our own history. If such things also happen in Karastra, then it seems the Far East is very much our kind of place. I see in the fact that Morand is now translated into German the operation of fate as well as a sure feeling for the petit bourgeois tastes of the German readership. It only took a very few lines of Morand to convince me that his Buddha is nothing but a German provincial potentate, and I can therefore imagine no apter purveyor of Eastern exoticism for Germany's literate households. The fact that Morand writes in French is just a pleasant way of proving to ourselves how easy it is to communicate with our neighbors.

That is the only reason—that, and because Morand's exceptional sales figures in France prove that literate households exist over there too—we are now taking this author more seriously than we would his German equivalent. This globetrotter, who, in a short spell at the wheel of a car, between one express train and the next, is able to knock out a worldview in a couple of thousand words, and who is capable, at a moment's notice, of pulling a globe out of his vest pocket—how did we ever get by without him! Before him we only had our doughty colonial travelers, who at least got their details wrong and had the inestimable advantage of not being able to write. Morand, though, can write: That is, he has the knack of being able to set down observations as if he had made them himself, and to conjure up, out of his narrow, American-cut sleeves a steady stream of fluent assertions. Nor does Morand content himself with details. On them, he bases a terrific line in generalizations. His Scotsmen wear kilts and have red hair. The keeper of a snobbish salon is "a gypsy," who is prepared "to scatter incense everywhere." The Soviet agent is inevitably a fat Jewish businessman with a briefcase full of propaganda leaflets.

His son is a Catholic priest in Paris. Morand couldn't have two Jews without pointing up the contradictions in the entire race. And on every page Morand's characters are representatives of race, nation, religion, estate, and type, so that one can flick through the books of this deft cosmopolite like the colorful pages of an atlas, where the people are as neatly classified and categorized as the dogs in a natural history textbook.

It's exactly the same with objects. In America, for instance, "the buildings rise vertically, like a shrill scream." London, meanwhile—how could it be otherwise?—is a veritable sea of chimneys. And even "the dead" are "lowered" into the ground—one really mustn't say "buried." The legs of a streetwalker resemble "a pair of scissors, cutting up the asphalt." The boldness of Morand's metaphors corresponds to the boldness of his world vision.

There is another form of solidarity, besides that of book-buying households. And in its name we would like to regret that other French authors are not translated instead of Morand. This solidarity even makes us wish we could protect France from its own Morands.

Frankfurter Zeitung, May 6, 1928

34

The Panopticum on Sunday

One day—it was a Sunday—the long-held reserve that kept me from ever setting foot in the Musée Grevin suddenly left me. It was raining at intervals. The clouds, which seemed to be made of sulfur, emitted a yellowish light. In the afternoon the people in their Sunday best came to look like defeated, ceremonial shades who had come to life for no purpose. It was as though the Sunday they had gone out to meet had been cancelled. In its place there was a kind of rainy, murky abeyance that separated the Saturday past from the Monday ahead, and in which the lost strollers were reeling about, both bodily and like ghosts, and all of them somehow waxen. By comparison with them, the wax dolls in the Musée Grevin were rather more accomplished imitations. The light from the yellow lamps in the windowless rooms, where daylight had never been allowed to penetrate, mingled so intensely with the darkness that loitered in the corners that they both seemed to be made of the same stuff—the light and the dark were siblings. The shapes of history and the confirmed authenticity of its faces, frock coats, costumes, top hats; the shadows that they cast on the floor in proof of their own true existence; the waxen immobility of their postures; and finally, the eerie silence that emanated

in equal part from living contemporaries and from the long
deceased—all seemed to me to be a pleasanter extension and affir-
mation of the yellow Sunday I had just escaped. Some characters
here had put one foot forward, their trousers were creased below
the knee in just such an unintended and inimitable way as the chin,
tripping over the hard edge of the collar, to form a double chin,
and there were a hundred little slovenlinesses on the part of nature
and the tailor that strove to convince the doubter of the genuineness of the figures here. Yes, the onlooker occasionally enlisted
himself and his own desire to be persuaded to support the intentions of the panopticum.

On the faces of the living visitors there was silence compounded
of awe, dread, and astonishment, which seemed to reflect that of
the figures themselves. No one dared to speak aloud. All were
whispering or speaking softly, as though they really were in the
proximity of important or frightful characters, and as though any
noise on their part could elicit an angry oath from the wax models. A smell of unaired clothing hovered round the exhibits, making them still more realistic. At the same time as the fear they
inspired, one felt a kind of sympathy with them, forever locked
away as they were, and almost resented it that their originals, those
of them who were among the living, were able to move and
breathe and act in the open air, and at the green tables of world
history. It was as though the real, the true Poincaré was standing
here in the panopticum, while the one who was at large, being
driven in some car to some official event or other, was the imita-
tion. Because all the most essential and characteristic attributes
seemed to have been taken away from the living original by the
wax model, leaving that to run around in the world without any
very firm identity or purpose. And, just as contemporary figures
seemed to have been filched from the earth, so dead heroes

seemed to have vanished from the beyond; and for the duration of my visit to the Musée Grevin it was clear to me that only mediocre shades could still be found in the underworld, in whom history and the Musée Grevin had expressed scant interest.

In Napoleon's death chamber on St. Helena one could smell the guttering light, even though it was produced by an electric bulb, and one froze in awe at the double silence of death, the metaphysical, and the imitated. Eternity was here captured for eternity, and the death angel's wings had lost their urgency, and were beating evenly, caught in the death chamber. Such objects as had authentically belonged to Napoleon, as, say, his watch, which lay on the bedside table, gave out an air of convincing genuineness, like the aroma given off by a spice or herb. Each little crevice between reproduced facts, into which the imagination of the onlooker might have slipped to make a nuisance of itself, was filled, with reproduced probabilities at the least. In which case the reality had not only been imitated, but exceeded. It was a world in which every physical appearance pre-emptively disarmed the human imagination, and where everything seemed to be physically there that otherwise one would hardly dare to try and picture with eyes closed. The shadows had become bodies, and cast shadows of their own.

The feeling everywhere was macabre. But it emanated less from the scenes of catastrophe (as, say, the persecution of the early Christians in Rome and the subterranean world of the catacombs) than the unremitting physicality with which everything had been imagined, the waxy hardness, surrounded by historically unimpeachable props, this whole unassailable history lesson, in which nothing could be doubted, simply because it was wax and could not be moved. It was like an encounter with occult phenomena, even though everything occult and hard to fathom was given a particularly thorough processing, and made available to all our earthly senses. One was given wonders to behold with one's own physical eyes, as a result of which one felt a little downcast and apprehensive about leaving this dear planet, where one had gone about so happily doubting and believing by turns.

It was only in one section—the Palais de Mirages, or Fairy-tale Palace—that the encounter with the miraculous was not awful but delightful. In this palace the ceiling and all the walls are of mirrors. In the middle of it are a couple of pillars, there not to support the ceiling so much as to scatter reflections of themselves. There is a special machinery there, of adjustable mirrors, which creates an incredible din when set in motion. To drown out this din, a mechanical organ plays opera music that seems to come from porcelain skies, brass spheres, and tin planets. For a while everything is pitch black. A pause, in which the excited senses get a moment to adjust to the next fairy tale, and for all male visitors an opportunity to grope the familiar bodies of their female consorts as if they were suddenly terrifically exotic in the dark. Then the lights of hundred thousand bulbs and lamps slowly rise, purple, yellow, green, blue, red, and we find ourselves in an Oriental palace supported on transparent columns. A few moments before, it had been densely leaved oaks and maples, and we had been in a French-German fairy-tale forest, with organ twitterings. Then there is the din again, and we are standing under a blue canopy of stars and comets.

It's not until they come to this palace that the spectators get over their whispered fearfulness and recover their instinctive love of show. Because, whatever improbable effects were realized, here too, thanks to the openly announced fairy-tale element, it remained a case of child's play, compared to the probabilities and actualities of human history. It felt not at all strange to be transported from the forest to the Alhambra in the twinkling of an eye. But what was impossible was the crucifixion of Christ, the death of Napoleon, the murder of Marat, the Roman circus. Yes, even contemporary politicians, whose achievements won't be truly ripe for the panopticum for another hundred years, already seemed improbable and ghostly, standing there in frock coat and top hat. I wonder how many of the spectators realized that it was themselves they were afraid of, and should have been afraid at later on in the streets as well—their own reflection in a shopwindow! There they all were, walking around, plaster and wax, with all the terrors of the panopticum in their own breasts, and each one's soul was a chamber of horrors. It was still raining, sporadically, slantwise; the yellow clouds were galloping over the rooftops; and a thousand umbrellas swayed eerily over the eerie heads.

Frankfurter Zeitung, June 10, 1928

35

The Child in Paris

There are children playing in all the parks. Walking on the grass is permitted to a degree that strikes the German visitor as practically sinful. And if there is something that grown-ups are not allowed to do in one or other of the city's great parks or little green spaces, then you can bet children will be allowed to do it. In Paris children are allowed to stand on benches, squeeze between railings, clamber over fences, throw balls into flowerbeds, and pluck flowers. The French are not the ones to apply Spartan principles of education. This people, that makes and bears so few children, not only respects the child as the future of the country, the nation, the world—it quite unthinkingly loves it, the child as creature, the becoming person who is still half an animal.

In the Jardin du Luxembourg, in the Champs-Élysées, in the Louvre—everywhere you look, there are little colored tents with puppet shows. The little audience sits on low benches, little girls like ladies, with gloves and hats; courtly little boys. Cavaliers with elegant gestures, who treat their ladies with consummate politeness and flawless manners. It's a fair reflection of grown-up French society. The culture of movement, of grace when walking, standing, or sitting, is something all these little girls have grasped as well as their young mothers. French children behave with the ease and confidence of grown-ups. It's not so much a matter of race and blood as it is the consequence of the warm, loving, nurturing softness in the way they are brought up. The French pedagogical principle is not Spartan strictness but Roman freedom accorded to the individual disposition—it's not discipline but civilization.

In parks and gardens, at every fair, in open spaces on particular holidays, there are carousels for children. Here is a game, a sport, that very subtly helps to train the child to be self-aware: The carousel owner has a stick in his hand with a number of rings on it. All the children, on their little rocking horses, in their tiny carriages, have been given a little catching stick. When they go past the rings, they try to catch one on their stick. Whoever has a certain number of rings gets a prize.

Even the very youngest, the three- or four-year-olds, play. They learn to reach out, learn the importance of the moment, quick thinking, good aim.

It's hard to think of a public park where strollers are not allowed on footpaths. Children are allowed to do everything: to rush ahead into museums and palaces, to feed swans, and sail little boats in ornamental ponds. You can buy these white sailboats in every toyshop, they are solidly built, with all the details of real sailboats, boats for Lilliputians. You let them tack across the large marble ponds, stand there on the shore for hours watching as the wind puffs out their sails, as the gentle current pulls the boats along, as two collide, as each one gets back safely to shore. Then you push them out again with long poles, on to the wide, sparkling circle of water.

Frankfurter Zeitung, March 17, 1929

36

Honor to the Roofs of Paris!

The French talkie *Sous les Toits de Paris** has been running in Frankfurt for several weeks now, and even though our colleague in the review section of the paper—quite rightly!—used the occasion of the Berlin premiere for a careful and comprehensive response to this exceptional work of cinematic art, still it seems to us to be worthy of another mention. It is our sense that repeated praise is called for to commend the noble discretion of this film to all those who, since the addition of sounds to shadows in the cinemas of European and American cities, are being forced to forget how expressive stillness can yet be, and how proverbially golden silence. But we don't really need this propagandistic sideline to cause us to raise our voice in praise of silence; even to give thanks, we should need to speak.

The action of this film emerges from the atmosphere of Paris in much the same way as a folk song is generated by a particular landscape. It's as though the tremulous, unresting fog over the roofs of Paris gave birth to the events that take place below. The

---

*Written and directed by René Clair, the 1930 comedy-drama remains a film classic.

thinning gray haze over a frisky tangle of chimneys in the opening
sequence of the film resembles a curtain that dissolves and turns
into the drama it has kept concealed hitherto. And when the drama
is over, it doesn't just end there, it's returned to the fertile fog from
whence it came and that is its true element. In the same way, certain vibrations are created in space, and return to space. In the
same way songs are created and then dip back into the world's
inexhaustible supply of melodies. The particular virtuosity of this
sound film is based on its use of the popular ballad—naturally, of
the same name—that runs through it, comments on it, begins and
ends it. The images seem to arise out of the stream of the melody,
even as it continues softly and gently to caress their edges. All the
old, collapsed, forever collapsing sweetness of lower class Parisian
life seems to emanate from these images: the joyful mustiness of
petit bourgeois life behind tall windows of slender, aristocratic
noblesse; the aromas of coffee and brandy in the cramped little
bistros, these pleasantest of dives, those bars that aren't dens of
vice but more fairy grottoes of vice. The smiling sweetness of the
little girls seems to overpower the dourness of their tough little
apache boyfriends; from ramshackle old walls, still standing only
by grace of some miracle, the old new life starts to glow; and a
conciliatory sun shines down on the hot-tempered fighters. An
accordion, the poor man's piano, sounds around the pleasant little
nooks of Montmartre. A beggar, hunkered down in a corner, is
handling it. He isn't really playing it, he's not the one eliciting the
long sighs of the lost from it, rather they seem to come from the
instrument itself, from its creased and pleated body, and if anything, the musician is more at pains to stifle them. But they, the
sounds, seem incapable of resisting the audience which has gathered around the singer and ballad seller, and they offer themselves
to each heart in the circle as a voice, an echo, each with its own

genuine, but suppressed sigh. And the off-key voices taking up the song, and the strident beauty of the instrument accompanying the singers as it seems to conduct the dance of the chimneys on the rooftops of Paris, together make up the sacred chorale of cheerful poverty. The singing, the accordion, the respectful listening, has had a cleansing effect on them all, enclosed as they are in the little square, which frames the verses of the ballad as tenderly as it does the ring of listeners. Even the pickpocket, shamefully but knavishly taking advantage of the dreaminess of the concierge's wife to empty her little purse, is tied to his victim by the music. It is not so much his theft as his betrayal of the community of listeners that offends our conscience. It's more a sacrilege than a crime that he commits: he has broken the reverent spell, violated the sacredness of the place and the occasion; he has offended against the religiosity of the "milieu."

See them sharing their last cigarette together, only to fly into an argument, and then to fall into one another's arms again! The tender pomp of the slippers the lover buys his girl! How many years of disgust and indifference in the bed of the concierge couple, and how much sweetness and sensuality in that first night of love for the young couple—too shy to use the bed, so they sleep on the floor! How much moving faithlessness in the little girl's little heart, when in her despair at her boyfriend's arrest during their honeymoon, she falls with his best friend—yes, falls! There is a fine, gentle falling in her life; she obeys the laws of gravity, which smilingly give her her orders, a charming, foolish creature, the most complete personification of feminine frailty. It's as though one could actually hear the thin, sinful voice of her red blood. She's falling, she's falling! She's in love, she's dancing, they're throwing dice for her, the pretty thing! Today she's conquered and tomorrow merely won. In her lovely little bosom are the stars of her destiny.

This sound film has all the charm of perdition. Not one of those playing here will ever leave this world. They will fall further and further into it, sink into the hill of years that come rolling up unstoppably, smiling, to the song of the accordion. Melancholy will always be a sister to their joys. They will always drink, love, throw dice, steal. Their fate is implacable. That's what gives the film its sadness. But the implacableness has a sheen of mildness, which makes it seem, as it were, placable. That's why it's such a joyful film.

Frankfurter Zeitung, October 28, 1930

37

The Frenchman
on Wotan's Oak

Georges Bernanos, French writer of distinction, publishes a book about the anti-Semitic publicist, Édouard Drumont,* who died in the war and had already been forgotten by the literary world; wrongly forgotten, because the polemicist Drumont was an important writer, of noble passions, forceful language, lethal wit, sparkling irony. His hatred was the hatred of a strong man, his love was warm and great, his personal courage (proved in many duels) was the source of his literary courage, his private life was of a piece with his public life, he truly was a knight without fear or stain, and the aim he followed with his life, with body and soul, sword and pistol, was, it has to be said, unfortunately extremely stupid: He wanted to exterminate the Jews. So much genius in the service of idiocy! So much bravery for weakness! So much nobility for an idea of savages. So much zeal for something so banal! So much Catholic faith for the devil, and so much prin-

*Georges Bernanos (1888–1948), author of *The Diary of a Country Priest* and other novels; Édouard Drumont (1844–1917), French journalist and anti-Semite. *La Grande peur des bien-pensants* was published in 1931, and contains such vile pieces of description as "strange little mannikins talking with their hands like apes," and "sitting over columns of figures, slavering like bitches in heat."

ciple for nothing! So much heroism for cowardice! So much insight for blindness: What a sorry waste of a life!

Even so: There can't have been many anti-Semites worth much in human or literary terms, and I'm certain Drumont has gone to heaven, to that section where the good cannibals sit, the handful of obsessives whose honesty is rewarded lest their stupidity be remarked. Bernanos, who also wants to save the great dead anti-Semite for posterity, seems to want to share the views of his subject and his master. But Bernanos is no polemicist but a novelist. He adopts a posture of piety when he should be adopting one of aggression. He has the bearing of a man following a funeral procession with drawn sword—when it should be lowered. He seems not quite to know what he should be doing, the novelist Bernanos: He fumbles and wails. The sort of thing that, according to the anti-Semites, the Jews are always doing. Bernanos's intentions are no less noble than the late Drumont's. But it matters less if a polemicist is naive: You forget the foolish aims if he has a good technique. But when a novelist gets his sword out and makes a naive impression, all you see is him hiding behind the other, as if behind a "big brother." I'm sure Bernanos must have as much courage as Drumont. But he is unable to handle the weapon he has borrowed from Drumont. So he finds himself in a position that is little better than a weakling's: he complains, and he swipes. His complaint is nobly made. His language has its own brilliance, and a loftiness that hasn't been heard much in recent years. He is an important writer. We are familiar with his novels (which have been translated into German): They are considerably better than the standard French productions of the past decade. They display understanding, conscience, tradition, and heavenly grace (in both the religious and the literary sense). In the book that he devotes to Drumont, he tries vainly to combine elegy with a call to arms; he doesn't succeed in giving the world a picture of the dead man, only an impression of him. This in turn seems to have been snatched from the jaws of oblivion—hardly an enduring memory.

The book announces its polemical intentions from the outset, in its title. It is called *La Grande peur des bien-pensants* (roughly, *The Great Fear of the Liberal Progressives*) and, in brackets, on the second title page, carries the name of Édouard Drumont in Roman type. The left hand lowers the flag, the right waves the sword. An appropriate way to honor the memory of a dead fighter—if you can do it. If not, it's best not to try. It would have been more worthy of the novelist Bernanos had he put the name of his hero on the first title page, and in bold face. (I assume, though, he followed the instructions of his publisher, who is the most vociferous in France: Grasset.)

Though this work has had a lot of attention paid to it, it would have remained a purely French domestic affair, and we would have had no occasion to concern ourselves with it, had it not appeared at a time when anti-Semitism is making great strides in Germany and seems to be on the point of going from cannibalism to parliamentarianism. At such a time it is important to learn: that a good Frenchman and a good Catholic blames Jews (especially Jews of German origin) for certain problems in France; that the French too have a weakness for blonds, and sometimes find themselves preferring a "Norman" to a "Celt" and a "Celt" to a "Mediterranean"; that a man can be capable of turning Catholicism into a private concern of the "French race," so that a venerable Catholic tradition is unable to prevent certain Frenchmen from creating their God in Wotan's image; and that blue eyes are favored among the French too, so there too is something the Germans don't have a monopoly on. Of course, we have every reason to admire the French, because their anti-Semites are so much more gifted than ours. What a pleasure it is, therefore, to hear that they are just as stupid! How satisfying to learn that an anti-Semite admired by the Catholic Bernanos laments the fact that Jesus Christ was the son of a Jew! This evidence that tasteless barbarity is not the exclusive preserve of one or two European countries will surely provide a basis for a future united Europe! Here's hoping! It seems that the French novelist, rather like the Slovak and Romanian peasant, believes in ritual murder. (Even today Bernanos believes that Dreyfus was guilty.) Bernanos is convinced that the only race fit to make the Catholic faith fruitful is the French. A French Catholic genius as the Nazi rector of Borkum is an interesting prospect. The ahistorical stupidity of relocating Rome in Normandy is barely distinguishable from the crassness of the German scholar and race theorist, who has gone looking for biblical paradise in East Prussia. We have nothing more to reproach one another for. We are even. France has its very own version of Thuringia!

This foolish provincial-messroom braggadocio, with which the courage of a dueling Jew is sneered at, while the conviction of anti-Semitic street gangs ("storm columns," they call them in Germany) that it is their sacred duty to smash in the heads or at least the hats of Jews comes in for a literary paean; this unexpected vulgarity that can yell "Yid!" without giving up its classical allure; this rampaging blindness swinging its cudgel and at the same time complaining in dignified language at all the harm done by those beaten; this loyalty to faith, aristocracy, heroism, tradition, nobility, all cheek by jowl with an adolescent desire for a fistfight; this hand that won't stop brandishing the knout while simultaneously aiming to make the sign of the cross; in a word, this whole mixture of crown and cross and swastika is a monster, eminently worthy of this period that Bernanos has it in for. How much he himself has become one of its defining products is something he will never realize.

There is more at stake here than a facile national satisfaction at the primitive fact that "everyone is going after their own Jews." I don't hesitate to call Bernanos's book dangerous, because in addition to being stupid, it also sanctions stupidity. It makes a difference whether a man supports his anti-Semitism with arguments drawn from Teutonic primal forests, or by calling Saint Augustine as his witness. What is unsurprising in a heathen becomes an act of godlessness coming from the hand and the pen of a man whose Christianity is beyond doubt, even though he may come from benighted provinces. Things one is used to hearing from the mouth of some godless S.A. goon who apes the posture and the inarticulacy of primitive thugs cannot be broadcast by a man who feels a mission to save Rome from the Jews, and the Messiah from his Jewish birth. The man who looks to the Edda for reasons why he should take from the Jews "their money" may be right. But the man who, Bible in hand, claims to have found there a text for the superiority of the "French race" is actually perpetrating a sacrilege.

No doubt Bernanos is aware of this, because he presents himself in the guise of a reformer, a "protestant" (in the literal sense). He rebukes the cardinals, and gives the pope plenty of free advice. He has no sense of the statesmanship, the care—the wisdom, even—that characterize the Vatican even when it makes obvious mistakes, and of the old, traditional gifts the institution hands on to its servants, seemingly automatically, and thanks to which the lowliest man in Rome's employ remains vastly superior to a—geographically and intellectually—provincial French novelist. Good old Bernanos is evidently hewn from the tough, decent wood that takes its descent from Wotan's oaks and that, for centuries now, has gone to make the founders of all "national churches." He is a schismatic. And, while he may have an appreciation of his hero

Drumont's sense of humor, he has none of his own. He fights against the Church with all the conviction of his feeling of being its "true son." He is quite sure that he is allowed to take certain "liberties." And he could probably get himself a kindly hearing, and perhaps even an occasional smile of approval, were it not that his ignorance makes it difficult for anyone to do more than forgive him. You have to say this for Bernanos: He's a menace to china shops; but in the fencing hall one can probably do better. He's one of the type of zealous Catholics who know better than the Church, and who are just about sharp-eyed enough to wag a finger at its crassest errors. There are banalities one doesn't mind with Drumont, because he's a natural polemicist—the only literary genre where banality is permitted. But what to do with the banalities of a novelist? What to do with idiocies couched in classic form and brilliant language, where the reader is delighted by the flair for language as much as he is annoyed by the pompous rectitude with which the author communicates his average insights? You forebear to laugh aloud out of respect for the author's literary credentials. But you can't repress a smile and a shake of the head.

But it's not a laughing or a smiling matter! It's a tragic sight! A distinguished man, a fighter for "justice and faith," sets out to fight this error, this hangover from the Enlightenment, this wretched mélange of godlessness and collectivism, the plebeian outlook that calls itself either "democratic" or "proletarian," and that fills literature and science and art with its dead weight, and drags them down with it. And in what armor does our champion step up? In that of National Socialism. With the pitiable delusion that he's got a cross on his knightly shield, and unable to see that his cross is showing vigorous signs of growth on all four ends of it, crooked excrescences; Bernanos is fighting under the swastika banner. He doesn't know that the idea of "race" and the idea of "anti-Semitism" are both sisters of nineteenth-century "materialism," companions and contemporaries of that crassness that took down the hero and set up the bourgeois in his place, substituted enlightenment for belief, the first cousin to the ape for the image of the Lord, the snooty bourgeois for the humble nobleman and noble humility. Blind and blond-besmitten, an "idealist," he's found the guilty party: the Jew, the trader, the moneyman, who buys and sells where others have to fight. This frightening ignorance that equates having dark hair with the stock market, and on the basis of individual "Levantines" claims the right sacrilegiously to interfere with God's purpose and deprecate Christ's origins—this ignorance is the clearest sign of "heathenism," the failed baptism, the voice of the great-grandfather in the bear's cave, of which Bernanos is so proud. When he applauds violent street criminals, he is his own club-waving ancestor. How can anyone who believes in divine mercy condemn a whole faith? And how can a man who condemns a faith *qua* faith not see that doing so puts him dangerously close to those "collectivists" of whom he disapproves? How can someone who can, at most, have met Mr. Arthur Meyer, the Western product of a barbarous religious persecution and a thoroughly European intellectual compromise, claim that he knows the Jews? This people whose mysterious Eastern masses—miles removed from any cosy, Western, savings-account mentality—are daily crucified, experience miracles, die of hunger, all for the God our anti-Semite claims to worship? Doesn't this French Catholic understand that he has far more in common with a Russian Hasid than with his own publisher in Paris?

He doesn't. Telling him is probably pointless. But I wanted to establish once and for all that anti-Semites have no place among the decent fighters for a return of human dignity. Anti-Semites belong on the other side. Petit bourgeois, materialistic, and low minded as they are, they have nothing to do with faith, heroism, and grace. Only a man who's desperately hard of hearing could confuse what he's pleased to call the "voice of his race" with the voice of heaven. But there are deaf Catholics too.

Der Morgen, August 1931

38

French People

ermann Wendel's latest book, *French People* (published by Rowohlt in Berlin), makes no claim, as the author writes in a foreword, to "instruct" the reader. "There is no particular intention behind these portrait sketches, they are just there." We take the author at his modest word while at the same time appreciating his literary courtesy. Almost an old-fashioned attitude, this gallantry toward a readership that by now probably won't understand it. Anyway, we should like to commend it. At a time when biographers are so sought after as writers that the facts or "facts" of their subjects' lives probably give them quite a comfortable living, it seems further meritorious to have assembled thirty-two portraits of interesting personalities in one volume, rather than, as the odd biographer would probably rather have done, fill thirty-two volumes and live off them for thirty-two years. Some of these subjects, admittedly, have quite a wide currency already. And if the author shows modesty in his foreword, then he shows as much courage later in not merely taking on such a much written-about figure as Joan of Arc but launching his book with that portrait.

Well, he doesn't have anything strikingly new to tell us about her, but in the overall context in which it appears, his portrait and the place it occupies are both of some significance. In fact, in the course of reading the book, the reader gradually comes to understand—I almost said, suspect—that the author's ostensible lack of any overall plan or concept is actually a front for quite a conceptual undertaking. The patent guilelessness of the title, *French People* comes to acquire an almost didactic weight. It seems, if you like, to have become detached from a sentence like: "You see, this is what French people are like!" or "Bet you didn't know French people were like this?!" In this way the book comes to acquire an unexpected, almost a contemporary-political message. Which is to say, in the case of a book written nowadays for a German readership by a German author who loves France: a humane message. And this is what our seemingly modest author has done. Whether discussing the journalist Severine, the intellectual great-granddaughter of Voltaire, or the blood-bespattered apostle of revolutionary cleanliness, Marc Guillaume Vadier, or the "veteran" Antoine de Lassalle, one of the most decent of those Frenchmen who inevitably call to mind the warlike traditions of Gaul, or poor Louis XVIII, or Louise Contat, the classic mistress of a period between epochs: everywhere—covertly, between the lines—the author is at pains to show the moral reasoning behind his book: namely, to make clear that some of his chosen representatives of the French nation have the so-called "manly virtues" like bravery, discretion, modesty, devotion, others have the expected charm, lightness, grace, etc., and a third group has both. The thirty-two figures that Wendel has selected from French history strike me as being a very sound representation of the "French national character," and I think one can learn a great deal about France and French charm and humanity from them. Over all the characters hangs a pall of melancholy. Death, with which each one of these minibiographies ends, casts its shadow over the life of this book. And so—because life is occluded by the shadow of death—the book comes to have a meta-physical gravity that contrasts with its historical levity. Yes, that seems to me to be its charm: that it is a description of death. Its value, though, is more practical: it teaches the reader about France, through representative individuals. Because it is only through its individuals that a nation can be known and understood.

Frankfurter Zeitung, July 31, 1932

39

Children Are Exchanged

As is generally known, there is a program involving the exchange of children between France and Germany. This has been going on for a number of years now. Before Hitler arrived on the scene, there was even a plan to set up a "Franco-German One-Year School," which had been due to open in October 1933 (simultaneously in Berlin and Paris). Hitherto the name of the administrative body in charge of this exchange program in Berlin was: "Society for Binational Education." Now—in other words, in the Third Reich—it will be called "Society for Student Exchange." At the head of this renamed society, we hear, there is to be not some fresh personality from the talented ranks of the nationalists but a former employee of the Society for Binational Education, an employee who, of course, has become a member of the Nazi Party. *The Third Reich is keenly interested in a continuation of the German-French student exchange scheme.* The Society for Student Exchange in Berlin "promises not to play politics." (But then, instead of three so-called summer camps planned for each country, there will now only be one.) Of the German teachers hitherto engaged at the German-French holiday schools, the majority have been dismissed. (No doubt they are Jews, or at least "Jews" as the racial laws define them.) No doubt either that those who have been dismissed have been the keenest proponents of "binational education" for the last few years. In France people know who they are. They know what they have achieved. In Germany, they know as well. And that's why they've been thrown out.

Well, the leading lights of the Society for Student Exchange in France have certainly *not* been thrown out. And those Frenchmen who previously had to deal with the true friends of France on this matter of the exchange of children will now have to deal instead with the enemies of the French people and of French children. They will have to deal with the bestial believers in the Third Reich and in that Hitler who wrote that the French race was negroid, Yiddified, and inferior. The innocent descendants of that race, meanwhile, will be kindly invited to visit the plague barracks and concentration camps of the Third Reich. What are they going to learn there? The German language? What, from newspapers like the *Völkischer Beobachter?* Or Hitler personally? Or his henchmen, men of the stamp of Goebbels and Göring? Or from the bards of National Socialism? Pity the generation that was given this Prusso-German instead of the language of Goethe! No, what the French children can learn in the Third Reich is this: to throw hand grenades, to spit at Jews, to despise Latin peoples (to despise their own people), to respect brutality, betrayal, injustice, and illegitimacy. No one who loves Germany would wish it to be seen by French children in this hour of its humiliation and darkness. And anyone who loves France would want to keep its children safe from the threat of having to learn the "Horst Wessel Song," to honor murder and murderers, to despise the cross and to bend it into the form of a swastika, to march in goose step, to blaspheme against God and mankind! . . . You don't send your children to plague barracks! . . .

Such is the generosity of the French people, so strong is its faith in the eternal and indestructible nature of mankind, that it's no surprise to see it, in all innocence, trusting in the eventual victory of humanity, continuing with the student exchange program, as if Germany were still Germany, the way France is still France, as if the language of the Third Reich were still a German language that one could and ought to learn—and not the barbarous stammering and whining it has become, a mixture of Prussian twaddle, German technical jargon from the small print in ads for eau de Cologne and shotgun pellets, and the sinister dysphemia of the old and the converted apologists of race and revolution.

As far as the "exchanged" German children go, who will spend a few weeks looking with startled, innocent eyes at a country where they don't bend the ends off crosses, don't spit at and murder Jews, don't put their socialists and pacifists in concentration camps; a country where you can go as you please, where you don't have to march; a country where the individual is respected, and the individual child treated with something verging on awe: these "exchanged" German children will find themselves back home a few weeks later, lined up in "shock troops," where they will hear from their teachers and trainers what a dissolute, Yiddified, negrified country France is: Which is no more than what Hitler wrote in his book, in black and white.

No, if French children want to learn German, there is a country where they've spoken good German since the days of Walther von der Vogelweide;* and the country is Austria. A country that was already German when in Brandenburg they were still speaking that Kashubian that today's Prussians have forgotten, without

---

*(1170–1230); Minnesinger and poet who wrote both love poetry and "political" works.

knowing the German they want to represent everywhere: no longer Kashubians* and not yet Germans!

So let people set up a Franco-Austrian children's exchange! In Austria the children of France will learn a true, a free German! And their young souls will not have to struggle with the terrible weight of having seen a country that smells of arson and murder: an un-German land.

Das Neue Tage-Buch (Paris), July 29, 1933

---

*West slavic language once widely spoken in Pomerania and West Prussia; some 200,000 speakers remain. Principally known in English through references in the work of Günter Grass, who was born in Danzig.

Part VI

In the Bistro After Midnight

40

God in Germany

S ince those heady days when the *Frankfurter Zeitung's* worldly
seeker-after-God, Friedrich Sieburg, thought he had come
upon Him in France, Germany's footing with the Almighty has
undergone a widely publicized change. Baldur von Schirach has
reintroduced Wotan—the undergod, his superior—proof of the
continuing health of the old Germanic gods. Hitler has kicked his
faithful Ekkehard, old Hindenburg, upstairs to Valhalla. Schleicher, the wicked Loki (once allied with the aforementioned
Sieburg, at the time when he was still looking for God in France
and a Chancellor in Germany) not having agreed to toe the line,
has been rubbed out. The Christian God, on account of His kin-
ship with Judaism, has been degraded to a second-class citizen at
best. He doesn't even have British or U.S. citizenship, even though
the *Times* or the *New York Herald* take up His case from time to
time. Since God, while omnipresent, is also invisible, it isn't possible to secure His expulsion from the Third Reich. But one may
assume—inasmuch as a poor mortal is capable of divining the ways
of the Almighty—that He turned His back on the leaders of the
Third Reich some time ago. Since the Christian faith is descended
from the Jewish, its priests and congregations suffer persecution.

But since the Regime has felt obliged to woo the Catholics of the Saarland, there have been recent attempts to offer a deal—a concordat—to God. The neoheathen naturally believes it is easier to put one over on the Almighty than on the Holy Father. But sometimes it appears that the sheep are more cautious and suspicious than the shepherd who has sat down to discussions with the wolf. God is held in low regard in Germany. But be assured that the Third Reich is even lower, in the eyes of the faithful.

It was crass and naive of the thinkers of the Third Reich to ban atheists and Freemasons and the Judeo-Christian God all at the same time. In the same way they dispatched Rosenberg, the *nagaika** diplomat from the Baltic, to London, and were only a whisker away from sending Baldur von Schirach to Rome. Those barbarians, who thought a gentleman by the name of Rosenberg would impress the bluebloods in London, when, at most he would be gawped at as an anti-Semite with an unlikely name—those barbarians would have been capable of assuming that Baldur could have signed a concordat with Pacelli, simply on the basis of being an opponent of the proletarian atheists. It seems almost like blind chance that it was von Papen who was sent to Rome. It took a long time before it was understood in Germany that banning atheists and persecuting Jews wasn't enough to qualify as a Christian state. When the pope sees a picture of Hitler, he—rightly—prefers the atheists. And as far as the Almighty is concerned, it's probably enough if He sees Papen, to prefer the atheist to the hypocrite.

No—neither the Catholics in Austria nor those in the Saarland will give credence to Hitler's sudden conversion. Even Hitler's fathers, those Germans who said they feared God and nothing else in the world, eventually suffered a crushing defeat. What about

---

*A *nagaika* is a whip, a cat-o'-nine-tails.

the people of the Third Reich, who are no longer afraid of God, but of everyone else, including even the Jews?!

The Third Reich will win only one victory—which it has already won: against the Jews. It's a victory against the children, the blessed, the accursed, of God. Before they came to power, those doughty heathens poured scorn on the "one-way street to Jerusalem." Well, now they have lost the Polish corridor, Austria, and (very soon) the Saarland, they will have only one success to celebrate: their victory over half a million Jews, the one-way street to Jerusalem.

It's time for Sieburg to write another book. I suggest he call this one: "God in Palestine, Wotan in Germany, Schleicher with God."

Das Neue Tage-Buch (Paris), September 8, 1934

41

Europe Is Possible Only Without the Third Reich

There is still—even today—a yearning, a nostalgia for European cultural solidarity. The solidarity itself no longer exists, except perhaps in the hearts and minds and consciences of one or two great men in individual nations. The sense of Europe—one might call it a "conscience of European culture"—started to fade in the years when a sense of nationhood awoke. One might say: *Patriotism has killed Europe.* Patriotism equals particularism. The man who loves his "fatherland," his "nation," above all else, has cancelled any commitment he might have to European solidarity. To love means to esteem—even perhaps to overestimate—the object of love. To love with open eyes, critically, is something only very few people are capable of doing. Most people's love is blind. Most people who love their fatherland, their nation, do so blindly. Not only are they incapable of seeing the faults of their nation, their country, they are even inclined to see its faults as instances of human virtue. This is called: "National self-confidence."

And yet: European culture is much older than the European nation-states. Greece, Rome, Israel, Christendom and Renaissance, the French Revolution and Germany's eighteenth century, the polyglot music of Austria and the poetry of the Slavs: These are the forces that have formed Europe. These forces have combined to form European solidarity and the cultural conscience of Europe. Not one of these forces was bounded by a national border. All are naturally opposed to the barbarity of so-called national pride.

The imbecile love of the "soil" kills the love of the earth. The pride of being born in a particular country, within a particular nation, wrecks the feeling of European universality. Either one can love all people equally or else one prefers one to all the rest. In other words one can be either a European or else a blind "patriot"—and most patriots are blind, are condemned to be blind, just as lovers are blind. If they weren't blind, they wouldn't be lovers.

I have been asked to say whether I believe that salvation for European culture is still possible. Of course I do! Even today!

At the considerable risk of being taken by your readers for an "unworldly utopian," I hereby offer you my prescription:

1. Some—still accredited, still repected—international forum should announce that every—and I mean every—form of "national pride" is stupid, and that any appeal to such a feeling constitutes poor taste.

2. The League of Nations in Geneva should declare that all people of whatever race are equal, and *any nation that disagrees should be thrown out.*

3. *And therefore Germany as presently configured—the Third Reich, in other words—should be denied the standing* of every other European country. Because, of all the countries and peoples of Europe, only Germany proclaims its right to a special historical destiny. *Germany should be quarantined: Then European solidarity will be*

restored. There is only *one* enemy of European solidarity today, and that enemy is Germany. That enemy is the Third Reich.

I IMPLORE READERS not to be too quick to accuse me of harboring some "resentment" or "hatred." Rather they should beware of that false "objectivity" that lead them to open their doors to murderers, lest these accuse their victims of having behaved badly.

I have no hatred for Germany; contempt, maybe. References to Germany's past seem absurd and laughable. Germany after 1870 is even more different from the old Germany than modern Greece is from classical Greece. There is no obligation to respect a Greek minister of today on the grounds that he was a compatriot of Pericles. By the same token, people should stop using the great German past as justification for hope in a great German future. Venizélos* has much more of Achilles in him than Goebbels, Göring, or Hitler has of, say, Hagen von Tronje.† It's a stupendous blunder to allow the German nation of today the credit—in spite of all its barbarities—to which its past apparently entitles it. They might tend the graves of Lessing and Schiller in their cemeteries, but that doesn't make them the heirs of Lessing and Schiller.

The Acropolis still stands in Athens. No one would dream of claiming that the Greek parliament of today is the heir to the agora of classical times. So why allow the Germany of today such credit as might have belonged to its traduced and repudiated forefathers?

A people who have Goebbels for their Lessing has rather less connection to the old Germany than the new Hellenes do with Agamemnon!

*Eleuthérios Venizélos (1804–1936), Greek statesman.
†Hagen von Tronje was one of the heroic characters of the Nibelungenlied.

There is *one* possibility, even today, of rebuilding European solidarity, and that is to exclude the "Third Reich" from European solidarity.

European solidarity is impossible with Germany, and with the "Third Reich." A Europe including such a Germany is a nonsense. *But without Germany, Europe is a force.*

Die Wahrheit (Prague), December 20, 1934

42

The Poet Paul Claudel

Among the handful of contemporary European writers who are more than merely talented, able, and gifted—namely, who have conscience—one would surely have to include Paul Claudel. In determining who is an important writer—one who not only depicts and shapes and articulates, but who has a vision, and can change things—conscience is the crucial factor. An author's conscience lends magic to his words, and only words endowed with magic have the ability to change or to renew the world. Conscience without faith is an impossibility. The conscience of a European writer is based on religion. Conscience lends magic to his words, faith makes them holy.

Paul Claudel* is a religious writer. Because he declares his faith in God, in the shapes he makes, the characters he draws, he relives, re-creates, the miracle of creation: in the literary and the religious sense. In major European literature, there is, I think, not one truly

---

*(1868–1955), French Catholic poet and diplomat, perhaps currently best known for appearing in W. H. Auden's poem "In Memory of W. B. Yeats": "Time that with this strange excuse / Pardoned Kipling and his views, / And will pardon Paul Claudel, / Pardons him for writing well."

living character that doesn't stand in the reflected glow of the miraculous creation of the first man. Every literary device, and every truly living character has the formal, ceremonial gleam of that very first earthly miracle. And since what sets man apart is the word, the divine breath, the only substance with which he can shape and create, the word also bears that formal, ceremonial, miraculous gleam.

It is typical of Claudel: the solemn phrase. He has an astonishing mastery of it (and moreover he loves it). He loves the full, orotund formulation. One could say of his sentences that they are both shrill and sonorous, like ambient bells. It is inevitable in a writer of Claudel's sort that, on occasion, in love with the iridescent depths of words, moved and enthralled by their magic, he sometimes becomes their victim. He serves and obeys the structure he himself built. But this is a sign of all true writers: They command language, and at the same time they are in thrall to it.

Dialogue is the form most congenial to Claudel. The wealth and the variety of his writing finds its aptest expression in this form. A German volume of *Thoughts and Conversations* (recently banned in the Third Reich) is one of Claudel's defining works. In this—by the way, exceedingly well translated—book there are his animadversions on all the big subjects—that is, everything of lasting, global importance. In modern parlance that would be: "all the problems of the present day." Politics, architecture, personal life, art, literature, society. The wisdom comes with humility, the solemn pronouncement always sounds engagingly apologetic, and the obligation of conscience always to have an assertion followed by its opposite has partly determined the form of the work. "For the writer," thus Claudel, "there is something alarming about the thought that for all eternity he will be identified with his collected works, that for all eternity he will be reminded of the misprint he neglected to correct— like a louse on his skin. . . ."

This humble and objective expression of writerly diligence and perfectionism gives some clue, perhaps, to the scale of his human responsibility, and his fear of God. Because when Paul Claudel says "eternity," one may be certain he did not mean merely to say "posterity," which for profane authors is the only heaven. He meant "eternity," the eternity of the beyond and of illimitable grace.

Der deutsche Weg (Oldenzaal), February 6, 1938

43

The Myth of the German Soul

I

Craven Western intellectuals have taken refuge in the myth of the "German soul." What put them to flight was the confusion of recent German history. Actually this history is less confused than the flight of those whose task it should have been to study and understand it.

There are certain parts of the world, well known to geographers, where the magnetic needle goes, as they say, haywire. That's no reason, though, to throw away the compass. Everything under the sun is subject to laws; which is not to say that there are no surprises. What would we have said of those explorers and scientists who, perplexed by the apparent failure of their needle, had made no effort to understand the natural causes of this failure? If they had given way to irrationalism, and declared that the compass itself had become "unfathomably mystical"?

There is nothing mystical about the fact that in certain parts of the world, the magnetic needle loses its orientation. Nor is there anything mystical about the fact that in certain nations, the intellect is regularly led astray. It is, as I say, a convenient excuse to claim that there is some exceptional irregularity at work. That excuse, like any dereliction, is dangerous. Still more dangerous is the way it encourages the myth of a problem's "unfathomable-ness," followed by the helpless "just nothing to be done about it" feeling with which one goes out to confront the "unfathomable."

The unfortunate myth of the German soul is not new—least of all in France, the country of reason, which has long been smitten with the irrational, and reckons to see a Walpurgis night in every wisp of German fog. No intellectual confusion is harder to correct than a case of collective intellectual snobbery. The "German soul" is finally defined as something indefinable, *et voila!* Historical facts are of as little use in correcting this as daily, hourly, current events. People have gotten used to viewing the shameful theatrical scenes that are produced in Germany from time to time through the same opera glasses they take to Wagner productions. In fact the West-ern diplomat and observer goes to Germany in very much the same frame of mind as the theatergoer gets into a taxi that will take him to see *The Ring*. This sloppy and snobbish laziness is sustained by mythology. Western politicians, diplomats, and journalists seem to be there in their capacity as Germanists rather than as politicians, etc.—and it's a curious fact that there are quite a few trained Ger-manists among them. Accordingly, they would much rather inter-pret the *Edda* than do what they're paid to do, which is to observe and explain contemporary events. They manage to view a common or garden janitor who has become a Nazi official, and is therefore sanctioned to murder for money, as a Fasolt or Fafnir or whatever; a failed painter and decorator as Siegfried*; a pathetic writer who had so much trouble with his pen that he was forced to turn his atten-tion to a helpless loudspeaker as possibly Loki.† In good postmen, who are forced to go to labor camp, they see a bunch of Nibelun-

*Hitler.
†Goebbels.

gen; Kriemhild is the foolish daughter of the delicatessen storekeeper who has to do kneebends in the Hitler Youth; and the instant they hear German radio, they are persuaded they must be hearing Richard Wagner's trombones. The equally mistaken or perverse view, held until a few years ago, of the "Faustian urge" of the German psyche, is gradually being replaced by the "Nordic" theory, with the word "dynamic" also often in attendance. I'm surprised they don't go all the way and interpret the brown shirts of the SA as bearskins.

This way of viewing the German scene is not new to the present rulers of Germany, and they know exactly how best to exploit it: both in their internal dealings with their population, and—more dangerous still—externally. They put up some Wagnerian scenery and give foreigners an operatic song and dance of their politics of vulgar expediency. They accommodate the romantic need of these foolish foreign observers to see the brutal, barbarous, straightforward murder of a worker or a woman "by the executioner's ax" from the point of view of a theatergoer. It's more comfortable that way, as there is something in human nature that would prefer to take brutality for a game. Then you either close your eyes to it or, almost as effective, you interpose a pair of opera glasses. One would rather interpret and explain, than see, watch, and observe. German history—German literary history too, for that matter—is full of gruesome material only waiting for the right poetic interpretation (even art may latterly have inhuman consequences).

It's not for nothing that Hitler admires Wagner's operas, or claims to admire them. I don't think it's a question of musical taste here. He likes their symbolism—a fake symbolism, incidentally—and their broad-brush politics.

Perhaps he doesn't like Wagner at all. Perhaps he's just come to be dependent on that inspired noisemonger as on that rather inferior one he's dubbed his own propaganda Wagner.

II

There's no doubt that a lot of the world's indifference toward the terrible things going on in Germany has to do with the European Wagner fixation. Straightforward murder is viewed as if it were happening under Bengal lights. The red blood that flows from the wound acquires a slightly distancing violet hue, and both murderer and victim look as though they're just waiting for the curtain to fall, to go back to the dressing room together to help each other clean off the pain, the wound, and the blood. The Germans have always had the gift of killing to music. Even that doesn't make them "northern barbarians," though. Under Frederick the Great the notorious practice of "running the gauntlet" involved the poor unfortunate delinquent running between two lines of soldiers with sticks, who were set to sing loudly in time to their blows, so that they, the executioners, didn't hear their victim's screams. This type of barbarism has as little to do with Nordic cruelty as with Nordic cunning. It doesn't come out of any *Edda*, it comes out of the Prussian army rule book. And the "atmosphere" flowing over the foreign guests at the Nuremberg Party rallies from the massive decor has as little to do with Hans Sachs—I mean the historical Hans Sachs, not the one in the *Die Meistersinger*—as the Berlin Kurfürstendamm has with Wotan, or as Baldur von Schirach, who has got himself invited to Paris to lecture on Goethe, has with the true—the mythological—Baldur, or with Goethe, or with Paris. The political terror that Hitler contrives to exert over his European colleagues is partly made possible by the world's unconscious—or at any rate insufficiently conscious—romantic delusion that some Herr Gustav Schulze from Magdeburg, who eats oatmeal when he has a gippy tummy, and liverwurst when he's better, must be at the very least some sort of Viking retainer. Yes, even the polyester uniform that Schulze has to squeeze himself into, has the advantage of looking like steel armor, by torchlight, and the poor journalist, who hasn't read his *Edda* or his Nibelungs or his Gudrun, but at least knows the fairy tales about the "Germanic soul," arrives in Germany completely prepared to discover in the wooden German that the German leadership speaks and writes, elements of the Old High German alliterative half-line. The Prussian symbolism matches the credulity of the Western Europeans. The machine spirit, the Prussian drill, has shrouded itself in German mythology. And what we call "the European world" has—as they don't say in Nordic—"bought it."

Das Neue Tage-Buch (Paris), March 12, 1938

44

Rest While Watching
the Demolition

Opposite the bistro where I've been sitting all day, an old building is being pulled down, a hotel I've lived in these past sixteen years*—apart from such time as I was away on my travels. Yesterday one wall, the back wall, was still standing, awaiting its final night. The three other walls were already rubble, on the half-fenced-off site. How oddly small the site seemed to me, compared to the big hotel that had formerly occupied the same space! You would have thought, too, that an empty site would appear bigger than one that was built on. But probably it's the sixteen years, now that they're over, seeming so precious to me, so full of precious things, that I can't understand how they could have elapsed in such a small space. And because the hotel is shattered and the years I lived in it have gone, it seems bigger in memory, much bigger than it can have been. On the one remaining wall I could still see the wallpaper in my room, which was sky blue with a fine gold pattern. Then, yesterday, they put up a scaffolding

*The Hotel Foyot, on the corner of the rue de Tournon, just off the Luxembourg Gardens. Whistler and Rilke stayed there, in their time, and there is a reference to it in Evelyn Waugh's *Brideshead Revisited*.

against the wall, and two workers climbed up on it. With pickax and sledgehammer they attacked my wallpaper, my wall; and then, when it was reeling and decrepit, the men tied ropes round the wall—the wall was to be put to death. The workers climbed down, dismantling the scaffolding as they went. The two ends of the rope hung down on either side of the wall. Each man took hold of one end and pulled. And with a crash the wall came down. Everything was obscured by a dense white cloud of plaster dust and mortar. From it emerged, all coated in white dust, like great millers who grind stones, the two men. They made straight for me, as they had been doing twice each day. They've known me since I've been sitting here. The younger one gestures back over his shoulder with his thumb, and says: "It's gone now, your wall!" I asked them both to stop and have a drink with me, more as if they'd been building me a wall. We joked about the wallpaper, the walls, my precious years. The workers were demolition men; knocking things down was their job; they would never think of building anything. "And quite right too!" they said. "Everyone does the job they do, and gets paid the going rate! And this man here is the king of the demolition men," said the younger one. The older one smiled. That's how cheerful the destroyers were, and I with them.

Now I'm sitting facing the vacant lot, and hearing the hours go by. You lose one home after another, I say to myself. Here I am, sitting with my wanderer's staff. My feet are sore, my heart is tired, my eyes are dry. Misery crouches beside me, ever larger and ever gentler; pain takes an interest, becomes huge and kind; terror flutters up, and it doesn't even frighten me anymore. And that's the most desolate thing of all.

Unimaginable things happen, and the hand remains calm and doesn't clutch at the head. On my right is the little post office; the postman comes out and delivers my letters, bad letters mostly;

when the hotel was still standing, he used to leave good letters on my table. A woman comes—one I used to love, and I smile, a shadow of an old smile I used to have, that I no longer miss. An old man shuffles by, wearing a pair of indoor slippers, and I envy him his shuffle and his being an old man. Boisterous customers stand around the bar, arguing. There is a series of unresolvable, albeit not-very-far-reaching differences of opinion between them on such matters as cigarette lighters, radios, racehorses, wives, makes of car, aperitifs, and other such weighty issues. A taxi driver walks in. The waiter brings him a glass of red wine. His taxi's waiting. The driver drinks his wine. Soon he's quite alone, facing the landlady across the bar. The waiter balances an empty can on a car tire. The guests laugh. They want me to laugh with them. Why not? I stand up, and I laugh. Who's that laughing in me? I've got misery waiting at my table, large, gentle misery. I won't be long, I'm just laughing!

Diagonally across from me is the barber, standing in front of his door, as white as a candle. Soon his customers will arrive, they will arrive at the end of their day's work, when the newspaper seller comes and brings me the evening papers, the ones that are full of heated skirmishes and cold blood, and that yet—one can't really believe it—flop rustling home on to the tables on the terrace like huge, exhausted peace doves at the end of their day. All the terror of the world is in them, all the terror of the whole grisly day, that's what makes them so tired. When the first silvery streetlights glimmer on, a refugee, an exile, sometimes comes along, without a wanderer's staff, quite as if he were at home here, and—as if he wanted to prove to me in one breath that he felt at home, that he knew his way around, but also that where he felt at home wasn't home—he says: "I know somewhere you can get a good, cheap meal here." And I'm glad for him that he does. I'm glad that he walks off under the trail of silvery streetlights, and doesn't stop, now that night is falling, to take in the ever-ghostlier-looking dust on the empty lot opposite. Not everyone has to get used to rubble and to shattered walls.

The exile, the displaced person, has taken the newspapers away with him. He wants to read them in his good, cheap restaurant. In front of me the table is empty.

Das Neue Tage-Buch (Paris), June 25, 1938

45

The Children of Exile

I

At a time when people are ruled by animals, and, perhaps in an effort to ingratiate themselves, band together to form animal protection societies, there is perhaps not a lot of sense in talking about children, much less the children of refugees. But it still seems to me there's a slight chance that a few people, even if they'd rather hear about parrots and sheepdogs than refugees, can't quite bring themselves to be indifferent to the plight of children who were driven from their cradles as their elders were from their homes. Perhaps it may not be an entirely futile undertaking to show that not all children have the traditional look of so-called "childish innocence"; their early encounters with the Medusa have given them a different look.

There are many occasions in my life—too many—when I get to meet refugee children. Sometimes I meet them in the waiting room of the police prefecture, where, after having walked so far, they get a chance to wait: wait for instructions, restrictions, objections, rejections, evictions. I have to say I like spending time in waiting rooms. Partly on account of the children, of course, but partly on account of the suffering I encounter here. The accumulation of so much grief makes it, so I've found, a little more bearable.

In the beginning, as I was first making myself acquainted with the sufferings brought on by our hospitality, I supposed that the children would know little or nothing of the misfortunes visited upon their parents. And it was on account of their ignorance and their unawareness that I felt sorrier for them than for their parents. It's a fairly easy matter to believe that an ignorant human creature, a child, in fact, with that fabled expression of "childish innocence" in its eyes, would suffer more than a grownup who sees and who knows. Then imagine my surprise when I came to understand that the children knew more than their parents! And then, how much more pain I felt on their behalf! Because—is there anything more painful than seeing *knowing* children? They know more than their parents. They see so clearly and pitilessly, that in fact it's the parents who seem to have a look of childish innocence about them. That should tell you something about the times we're living in! The children know—and their elders beside them seem to have no idea. No idea how they fell into the clutches of their terrible destiny, and there beside them are their knowing children, whose disillusioned eyes seem past the point of expressing accusation, and are already offering them forgiveness.

I would like to flesh out what I was saying by relating a little conversation I had with the eight-year-old son of an Austrian shoemaker in the waiting room of the police prefecture. The father was summoned into the office in order to be instructed or obstructed or evicted or rejected. He asked me to watch his little boy while he was gone.

II

"Can you speak any French yet?" I asked.

"Just about," he said, "I've already been here three months."

"Would you like to stay?"

"I don't know. I'm not the one who decides."

"Why did you leave Vienna?"

"Because of the race laws. My mother's Jewish."

"Then why didn't your father divorce her?"

"He loves her. So do I."

(*Long pause, followed by*:)

"It happens."

"Did you see the Führer?"

"Yes!"

"How did you like him?"

"Are you a spy?"

"No! I've come here with your father."

"Spies could do that, too!"

"I'm not a spy."

"That's what everyone said in Vienna, even in in Ottakring, where we lived."

"What would you like to do?"

"I'd like to shoot!"

"Shoot who or what?"

"Snoopers."

"Where do you find them?"

"Everywhere! You might be one, too."

"Would you like me to take you to the circus?"

"No! Got no time for the circus!"

Just then, the father, the shoemaker, the man who—miracle!—loved his wife, came out of the policeman's office. He had received nothing worse than an instruction, no eviction. He was joyful. In his eyes there was that "childish look of innocence," that look that, as soon as it shows in the eyes of an adult, enjoins them and condemns them to folly.

He shook my hand and thanked me for going with him to the police prefecture. All at once, I had the feeling I should tell him: "Now, you be careful! Always let your son take you by the hand!" But instead I turned to his son: "Now, you look after your father! Don't let him out of your sight for a moment!"

"I know, I know!" he said. And he waved to me, small and slight, a little slip of a boy—and already an old man.

III

I've just seen a photograph, printed in several newspapers, of a little English girl who apparently had been waiting since ten in the morning for Neville Chamberlain and his wife, and finally got to meet them in the afternoon, and, on behalf of all British children, to express her thanks to the British prime minister for going to Germany on his peace missions. A sweet little English girl.

God grant that she never comes into the sort of knowledge that the eight-year-old son of my Austrian shoemaker has come into.

Die Zukunft (Paris), October 12, 1938

46

In the Bistro After Midnight

The clientele of the bistro, where I sit every night past midnight, is mostly made up of the so-called little people of the *quartier*: postmen, who have been on their feet all day; policemen, who are about to go out on night duty, and have just come in to drink a black coffee with kirsch (because it isn't just a matter of staying awake but also of being in the mood to stay awake). Waiters on their way home from work, actors whose theater has just closed after the performance, and one or two stagehands from the same theater, taxi drivers whose stand happens to be just outside my bistro, and also one or two chance passersby, who really meant to do nothing more than step in to buy a pack of cigarettes, but—charmed by the good humor and animatedness of the customers at the bar, and the colorful array of drinks standing in front of them, have stopped at the bar, and, having wanted to do nothing more than buy a pack of cigarettes—bought themselves a drink and joined the conversation.

We locals view them slightly askance. For many years we've been meeting at this bar every night, and we've come to feel like travelers who've been sharing a train compartment for a long time when suddenly some strangers come in. In spite of that, one or other of the newcomers manages to win us over, to the extent that, following a brief hostile silence, the conversation is resumed, almost like a piece of music after a pause. Nothing encourages us more than the sudden perception that the gate-crasher, having blundered in from some other *quartier* to buy cigarettes, would actually qualify quite well for life here with us. Having established, by a consensus of looks and nods, that he is entitled to remain at the bar, we pick up the threads of our conversation again.

Here, I reproduce, more or less verbatim, an excerpt from one of our nightly sessions:

The postman, a slight fellow on quick feet, as befits his profession, spoke first: "I tell you, it'll all come to a bad end, if the world carries on the way it's headed. Look at us, standing here over our drinks; who knows whether we'll still be around to do this in a year's time?"

"But without a question," said the man who looks like an accountant; in other words, calm, certain of his pension rights, knowing he has a little money tucked away in the bank, and yet bothered by a vague fear that it might somehow evaporate. His optimism was not the expression of his confidence, but more an attempt to soothe his own fears. "Things will settle down now. I'm not worried."

"I am," said the stagehand. "Death scares me. We won't be able to go on standing at the bar and drinking. But even more, life scares me. I'm even afraid of this moment, now, as we're standing here happily over our drinks. I have this feeling we're not really happy. If you were a stagehand like me, I'm sure you'd have exactly the same feeling. It's the feeling that our lives are a play. Third act, I should say. Maybe Monsieur B. knows what I mean."

B., an actor in the same theater where the stagehand worked, gave an unconvinced-sounding "Um." He hadn't been listening.

He fancied himself as a matinee idol. He thought, therefore, that a single "Um" coming from him, spoken, not to say declaimed without conviction, had considerably more weight than the excited speeches of the others. Perhaps he was also a little offended that the others had been given so many lines. Because he listened only to his own inner hollowness, it was only those mute voices within him that he attended to.

"Well now," said the night waiter, "when you talk about the world, it all depends on what you mean. The world you're talking about consists of just a handful of people. They direct the affairs of the whole planet. The fate of the planet is in their hands. Who knows what private interests they may have? A minister's not just a minister, is he? A minister's a human being, too. He's got a wife, a mistress, a son. Who knows what makes him decide something one way or another?"

The two policemen, meaty, feisty, almost seeming to burst out of their uniforms, spoke together: "That's the way the world is. Strictly off the record, of course." Thereupon they ordered two more coffees with kirsch (they got a special rate—mildly special).

"No politics," said the gentleman who looked like an accountant. He paid and got up to go. But in the doorway he ran into our old taxi driver, whom he hated. So as not to betray the fact, he turned back inside.

The driver comes to our bistro every night. If it wasn't that he was already so advanced in years, you could call him our golden boy. In fact he was so advanced that we thought we'd never catch up to him. All his life he had been a coachman. But then, when the human age for horses, the era when the equine race was involved with the human race, came to an end, he had become a driver. It's a miracle that he still is. Because just as he might once have been in the habit of allowing his horses to drink at every fountain, so he himself now, possibly in melancholy tribute to these long-since-slaughtered beasts, was in the habit of taking a drink in all the bistros and bars he happened to pass on his journeys. It was a miracle that he had been able to join us so late at night. But it was a regular, almost a nightly, miracle. As usual he spoke up at once, and what he said was this:

"Don't you go losing yourselves in these trivialities! Don't talk to me about politics. I know why the world is coming to grief, because I used to be a coachman. It's conscience—gentlemen—concience has been eradicated. It's been replaced by authorization. It used to be that every man had his own conscience. And he behaved accordingly. Even my horses had a conscience. Nowadays, here's an example from my working life: You're perfectly entitled to run someone over, so long as he's not on a pedestrian crossing. When a customs officer on the border drags a blind or a handicapped passenger out of his compartment and subjects him to a search, there's not a trace of conscience in the customs officer. He's not just got his authorization, he has his empowerment. And yet the customs officer's only human. The minister is authorized to negotiate on behalf of his people. His authorization kills off his conscience. As for dictators, the only mystery there is that they've given themselves their own authorization. They don't just want to silence conscience, they want to kill it off. And so they have! The governments in democracies only want to silence it. And they've done that too! With authorization to follow. Horses are what I know, gentlemen! Every horse would hesitate when someone ran across the road in front of it. My taxi doesn't hesitate. My horses had a conscience. My car has an authorization. That's where I see the distinction. In my day, when I was still a coachman, even a diplomat used to have a conscience. Today, now that I'm a driver, even a member of parliament only has powers.

"No more conscience in the world! No more horses!"

And so he ended his speech, and everyone laughed. They thought he'd had a few—which he had. Anyway, it's typical of people today that when they're drunk and they hear the truth and they recognize it, still they try to tell themselves it's only the wild talk of someone drunk like themselves. The two meaty policemen left. From the Senat, it struck two o'clock. And the landlady said: "Time for bed, gentlemen." And she started putting the chairs on the tables. It looked as though, at nighttime, the chairs got to ride on the tables.

Die Zukunft (Paris), November 11, 1938*

*This article ran during *Kristallnacht*, the pogrom throughout Germany in which synagogues were burned, Jewish businesses vandalized, and Jews beaten and killed. It was written at about the time (November 7) a young Jewish émigré from Poland, Herschel Grynszpan, shot and killed Ernst vom Rath, first secretary of the German Embassy in Paris. The Nazis used the attack as the "reason" for the pogrom.

47

Old Cossacks

I t was twenty years ago that the troupe of singing Cossacks came out of Russia. I knew them. The first place they came to was Berlin. Then they played in Vienna for a couple of weeks. After that I saw them in Zürich, then in Belgrade and Bucharest. Their fate, the fate of touring musicians, which is settled for them by concert agencies, took them north, to Prague and to Copenhagen. Then they went to London. From London to Paris. They were young, healthy Cossacks, in white silk *rubashkas*, with Cossack belts and topboots. Each of them played a different instrument, and they could all play every instrument. They were professional singers and musicians, but for business reasons they had to call themselves Cossacks. Only a few of them were descended from actual Cossack families. Fine feathers may or may not make fine birds, but songs make Cossacks, and my singers sang and played in a way that even the originals on the banks of the Don couldn't have improved upon. They had homesickness in their hearts and in their throats, and in their obligatory balalaikas. They were among the earliest victims of a world that was just beginning to make people stateless, and things hadn't yet gotten really tough. Furthermore, my Cossacks had the hope that "things might change." So they lived with one eye on the past, from day to day, hoping that each day might bring them a different future. They understood nothing of politics. They had been the professional musicians for an exiled public, and had simply followed their audience abroad.

There were women among them too, young and strong. In the mornings they looked like melancholy Russian girls; they had wide, beautiful faces, whole landscapes of faces. You could stroll about in them with your eyes. But in the evening they were princesses in blue dresses, with little silver diadems in their hair and silver slippers on their feet, which peeped out from below their long skirts like little sparkling precious stones. They traveled from town to town in reserved compartments, but they were third-class compartments. It wasn't really traveling, it was more that they had themselves forwarded.

A couple of days ago I ran into them again. The concert agency had dispatched them to Paris again, them and their balalaikas and their blue dresses and their little silver diadems and their silver slippers and their white *rubashkas* and their Cossack belts. The women wore more makeup, more powder, more undergarments, and the men's boots were just as shiny as ever. But how tired the feet were in their boots, the much-traveled feet in those carefully looked-after boots! And the Cossacks' faces had gotten pasty. And twenty years is a long time! Homesickness makes people age, and all hope was gone. . . .

A new wave of refugees has arrived in the city. You and I, for instance, with a pain that's twenty years fresher. And our destinies will be haggled over in ministries rather than in concert agencies. But we too will be going on a lot of "tours" that one would have to be a real Cossack to survive.

Pariser Tageszeitung, January 20, 1939

48

From the "Black-and-Yellow Diary," Entries from March 12 and 13, 1939

March 12[*]

There is an impoverished Austrian cabaret in Paris that goes by the name of "Mélodie Viennoise." It lives off the scanty resources of its exiled compatriots, and was closed on the evening of our day of mourning. Austrian entertainers—desperate men and women, in other words—sing and play and dance there. I don't know whether I'd be able to appreciate their art, but tact is an important, perhaps even a decisive, part of all art; Austrian art in particular. And the fact that this cabaret spent part of its certainly not very plentiful budget on placing advertisements in the newspapers to the effect that they would be closed on March 11, is more than a gesture: it's a small but distinct sacrifice. "There's a bit of an artist in every Austrian." That was said by, of all people, Friedrich Hebbel,[†] the genius of the heathland and implacable

---

[*]March 12, 1938, was the date of the *Anschluss*, the annexation of Austria to the Third Reich.

[†]Christian Friedrich Hebbel (1813–63), German poet and playwright who left his provincial Holstein for Paris and then Vienna, where he found his great success.

Protestantism, blown to Vienna by the north wind. I'm almost inclined to think that every desperate Austrian is a whole artist. I don't as a rule like cabaret. But this one I think will be art.

March 13

The journal *Nouvelles d'Autriche*, in one of its recent editions, has been looking into the phenomenon of royalism, in its section "Echo of the Month," which is signed by one "Audax." The pseudonym is fitting. Because it takes audacity to write without any talent, and to offer opinions without any taste. "Audax," then, writes as follows: "The Austrian community in Paris—there must be at least eighty of them—were recently informed by the *Paris-Midi* that they were to have met 'their emperor' in a gallery in the highly prestigious Faubourg Saint-Honoré." The community, Audax goes on to say, would certainly have been apprised of the existence of one Herr Otto Habsburg-Lorraine, but the sudden restoration of the empire would have taken them unawares. Note the delicious light-handed irony of our hack, who thinks that by calling the Faubourg Saint-Honoré "prestigious," and calling the heir to the Austrian throne "*Herr*," he can undermine the royalist cause. Audacity alone probably cannot confer the ability to determine what is "prestigious" and what isn't. Being of a less venturesome disposition than "Audax," I am loathe to say whether the rue de l'Ancienne Comédie, where the *Nouvelles d'Autriche* has its offices, is any more or less prestigious than the Faubourg Saint-Honoré. One thing I am able to say, though, is that the Faubourg Saint-Honoré would suffer a considerable loss of prestige if the *Nouvelles d'Autriche* were to move its seat there, and Audax were to live and scribble there.

I note, though, rather to my surprise, that crass insolence does not exclude incompetence. Because with that unprincipledness that, in the opinion of the audacious Audax, is an exclusive preserve of the wealthy and prestigious, the editors of the *Nouvelles d'Autriche* include on page 77 of the same issue, a notice of the exhibition that the emperor had attended; in which notice one may read: "It is some small consolation to learn that a Viennese citizen has succeeded in salvaging some valuable paintings from his erstwhile gallery in Vienna. Some of these paintings . . . are currently on show . . . in a small exhibition in the Faubourg Saint-Honoré."

What is sauce for the goose on page 77 ought, one thinks, to be sauce for the gander on page 45.

Meanwhile it affords us some small consolation to learn that the editors' left hand seems not to know where the right has been grubbing.

Die Österreichische Post (Paris), April 1, 1939

49

Clemenceau

(abridged version, 1939)[*]

Funeral Oration, by way of an Introduction

This extraordinary man, who died so—too—many years ago, left instructions in his will that he wanted no formalities at his funeral. He was accordingly buried at two in the morning, in the rain, and only his immediate family was present. Today, after many years and many, many works written in his memory, to write an obituary of the man no longer seems to me to disrespect his last wishes. The question as to whether, as a non-Frenchman, one is entitled to write such an obituary seems to me spurious, at a time in which many people all over Europe are lamenting the passing of Clemenceau's inheritance—yes, more than its passing, its destruction, its deliberate destruction. And while the deceased may have made one or two crucial mistakes, thereby making it eas-

---

[*]Georges Clemenceau, 1841–1929, was the subject of a 50-page monograph that vies with *The Legend of the Holy Drinker* for the honor of being Roth's last work. His ever-clearer hatred of Germany seized on the French statesman and patriot as an unlikely, even tragic, subject of identification. Katharina Ochse's abridgement concentrates on the Franco-German issues of the life.

ier for his enemies, the enemies not just of his own country but of the whole civilized world, to accomplish their destructive work; and while it may have fallen to us, in the course of this brief monograph, to point out these mistakes, yet our respect for this immense character compels us to express our unmixed regret at the destruction of his inheritance. We are further compelled to do so by our conscience as a European, a conscience further sharpened by our affliction as a suffering European. This is one of the very rare instances where morality calls for an "original" quotation, and where we must bring to a forgetful world the understandings of the aged Clemenceau, which are applicable yesterday, today, and, I'm sorry to say, tomorrow too. Yes, it is an urgent task not just to speak over his grave, but, as it were, to let the grave speak as well: What is this "Germanic civilization"—Clemenceau asks himself—this monstrous eruption of a will to power, that *openly* threatens to destroy the various accomplishments of progress, merely in order to establish the implacable rule of a single race, whose drive to hegemony sets its own armed force ahead of the development of all nations? . . . I am not about to prosecute Germany. There's nothing I desire more for my fatherland than peace with Germany. But for a lasting peace to be possible, both parties must have a similar interpretation of the law, and an equal capacity for good will. Too many men in public life, dazzled by their inordinately high opinion of themselves, have failed to see the problems of establishing lasting peace. . . . Whether we like it or not, it won't be the international parliament in Geneva that establishes future peace. . . . The American solution to the problem of war reparations owed to the Allies can influence the debate on the future course of the world, decisively, and for ill. . . . They are all there, from the international lawyers of Germany to the poets, in a phalanx, to make their appeal to the conscience of the peoples of the world. . . . The Treaty of Locarno offers merely the illusion of security: It is an illusion designed to deceive the inattentive and to lull the alert. . . .

Is the voice from the grave not speaking loudly enough? Is it only speaking to France? Is only a part of the still civilized world committed to listening to it, and is only a part entitled to give it a response? Is this voice not that of humanity in every language, of every country? Have these words from the grave not been sufficiently borne out? And while the deceased might not have asked for eulogies to be spoken over his fresh grave, is it not manifestly his intention that there be no end to a remembrancing of him, with his grave long grown over? Europe, inasmuch as it breathes and lives at all, chatters or is silent, and only from a few isolated graves is its truth still spoken. It is about to become a cemetery, because it paid insufficient attention to its own; a mass grave, because it did not honor its graves; it is about to die in fear, because it has failed to show respect. An old man, a stern man, a triumphant man, endowed with a clear-eyed hatred, as though chosen by nature itself to safeguard the goods of man, writes day after day, night after night, at his autobiography,* which is a warning, and he is forced to confess that his caution was not enough, his protective measures insufficient, his suspicion during the victory celebrations not wakeful enough, and the triumph was premature. And this man, the most parsimonious user of language, whose mouth never spoke an idle syllable, whose every written word served an aim and a purpose, people now listen to with half an ear, unpersuaded, or read inattentively or not at all. There is no one now alive who is shaken by the tragic vision of a man who all his

---

*In the Evening of My Thought, published in 1929. (He predicted another war with Germany by 1940.)

life was self-righteous, always ruthlessly unforgiving of negligence, a driven swordsmith, the only tireless lookout as the forces of evil approached, and then, once they were there, the most obdurate defender of military might and the most implacable fighter for victory; no one now alive is shaken by the late insight of this already very old man that he might have built up defenses in some places that didn't need them, and might have neglected to defend others that did. Even he, one of the almost infallible ones, wishes it to be known that he is prone to error, and to weakness! But all these warnings are cast aside.

That's why anyone who would like the voice of the dead man to be with us, and heard by us a little longer is entitled to speak at the grave of this man. The voice not only speaks French, it speaks European, it speaks human. We should attend to what it says.[. . .]:

The Ancestral Enemy

[Joseph] Caillaux had drawn up the treaty with Germany that was to fix the boundaries between the French and German possessions in Africa for all time. In 1911 the German gunboat *Panther* was sent to Morocco. Disturbances had broken out in Fez. France was forced to intervene. For a few days, war seemed imminent. Caillaux signed the Treaty of Agadir. In February 1912 [Raymond] Poincaré was the Prime Minister, the Senate was to debate the treaty.

Clemenceau spoke roughly as follows:

> This treaty, here before us to be ratified, was negotiated under threat from the German guns at Agadir. I don't believe it guarantees us a lasting peace. If I did, I would vote for it.
>
> During the last decades of the nineteenth century, we have seen that there are many very deep differences and oppositions

between France and Germany, moral oppositions. I speak without hatred; with its victories in 1866 and 1870/71, Germany has changed the European balance of power. Our Napoleonic troops may not always have been easy to live with. But our style of occupation and of victory is different. Our armies were welcomed in every city they went. When Bismarck wanted to take Paris, we were afraid he would raze it to the ground. We did everything we possibly could to prevent him from occupying it. At the time, our [Jules] Favre said to Bismarck: "Is there not enough glory for you in having conquered Paris?" "The word *glory* doesn't cut much ice where I'm from!" replied Bismarck. What glory signifies to us, power signifies to the Germans. In '71 only the Catholic Church remained upright. All other social and political bonds were torn. It took the Republican Party to put the country on its feet again. Today France is once more capable of fighting and winning. The idea of making overtures to Germany comes from financial interests, which are not responsible for our national foreign policy. We have been conquered, but we have not been humiliated. If we fail to ratify the treaty, that will mean a step into the unknown. But if we do ratify it, that is a step into the all too well-known.

We would like to quote two more passages directly from the speech:

One day, the 'duck's beak' and the "*Griffe des Omars*" will grow out; one concession will always lead on to the next. I don't believe in a politics of least endeavor. There are hours, in the lives of men as in the lives of nations, in which one must say: "Herr Bethmann-Hollweg* won't be happy!" Well, so he won't

*Theobald von Bethmann-Hollweg (1856–1921) was German chancellor from 1909 to 1917.

be happy. . . . The British think this is an excellent treaty. So
they should. We free them of the German presence in Morocco
by letting Wilhelm II walk off with a French colony.

The Senate ratified the treaty. And—until the outbreak of
war—its provisions were strictly observed.

Clemenceau was the only French statesman and politician of
the period to have *understood* the new, Prussified Germans; others may have *known* them. . . . It's practically taken for granted in
the West that the way you come to know a country and its people is by learning the language, living in the cities, touring the villages, the forests, the streets; especially by managing to speak to as
large a number of individual citizens from as many different back-
grounds as possible. It transpires, however, that there are some
peoples whose habits, customs, national, political and social forms
change so frequently that a foreigner who returns to the country,
say five years after having, in his view, thoroughly gotten to know
it, is compelled to start over. Most students of foreign countries
only have an eye for those attributes of a people that traditionally
are deemed to be its "distinctive traits": such things as language,
costume, habits, landscape. All this is applicable—relatively applicable—in countries that have a settled character, a stable energy,
a linear development, and personal liberty for the individual.
Even if Clemenceau had never set foot outside the offices of the
Homme libre, he would still have done more for the assessment of
Germany than his compatriots who studied German in Göttin-
gen, stared at gabled houses in Nuremberg, celebrated Pomeran-
ian Christmases, and became embassy first secretaries, military
attachés, and foreign correspondents. There can be no "lasting
peace" between a Prussian Germany and France, there can only
be short-term arrangements. If Prussia should even one day cease

to be the "ancestral enemy" of France, then there would still be an ancestral suspicion between the two countries, if you like, in place of a live frontier. In the space of just seven centuries, German habits have changed decisively, and German landscapes changed out of recognition. Even though they haven't moved, they look as if they've been on a long journey. The German people have made themselves new mother tongues on no fewer than three occasions, the latest of them resembling the earliest about as much as a sixteen-year-old girl resembles her ninety-year-old grandmother. What has remained constant has been a couple of latent qualities that cannot be arrived at with the help of a knowledge of language and ethnology. In fact they are not to be "arrived at" at all. One may perhaps infer their existence intuitively. One needs to be in a particular condition, less influenced by external appearances, as is sometimes produced by hatred or fear: in the condition of the clairvoyant or the clairaudiant. Some of Germany's periodically conquered neighbors sometimes find themselves in such a condition; for instance, the Poles, the French, the Austrians; these last in particular, because they have two traits that help them to beware of the Germans: First, they share one language, and are thus immediately able to hear the least threat to themselves; and second, they have a different character. And are therefore in a position to know themselves at risk, with complete clarity and insight. The statesman, who made not infrequent errors but only rare mistakes, must carry the blame for the worst of these; it was the worst because Clemenceau made it against himself. It was the mistake of using a peace conference as a place to settle a grudge; the typical mistake of his deep, almost animal vitality.

The Leap of the Tiger

On August 4, 1914, Clemenceau buried Jean Jaurès,* the first victim of the World War. His presence there made the occasion symbolic. If Wilhelm II said that for him there were no longer political parties, only Germans, then—apart from the fact that he was lying—he was plagiarizing the tacit resolve of the Gallic Clemenceau. For Clemenceau there were no longer enmities, there was only France. And of course there was Germany as well.

Here are his words, published in the journal he edited, the *Homme libre*:

> And now to arms! Everyone. I have seen men weep because they can't be present at the first engagements. Everyone's turn will come; there is no child on the planet that does not belong to this great battle! Dying is nothing; we must *win*. For that we need an army of everyone. Even the weakest will share in the glory. *One* nation: that is *one* soul.

And the following battle cry was heard:

> We come before you with one thing in mind, total war, no more pacifist campaigns, no more German prevarication, no betrayal and no quasi-betrayal! Our armies will not have to fight between two fires . . . The country will know that it is at war, and being defended. . . .

*Jean Jaurès (1859–1914), socialist depty, outspoken anti-war leader; he was assassinated on July 31, 1914, by a nationalist fanatic.

And this prediction:

> One day, waves of tumultuous enthusiasm will receive our vic-
> torious banners, our bloodstained, tear-soaked, shell-torn ban-
> ners, a wonderful tribute to our great dead. To bring about this
> day, the greatest day of our history; it is in our power.

At first the Germans are winning. The French retreat in the north.
Prime Minister [René] Viviani wants Clemenceau in his cabinet.
Clemenceau prefers a critical free role on the opposition
benches—either that or the prime ministership, nothing in
between. He wants sweeping reforms in the army and the administration. He wants the plain truth reported from the front, no
deceit, no lies. The first serious, bitter quarrel erupts between
Clemenceau and Poincaré, the president of the Republic. It her-
alds a long enmity, which will continue till Clemenceau forms his
war cabinet. The government is in Bordeaux, Clemenceau is
"Président de la Commission de l'Armée," the scourge of the general staff, the protector of the front-line troops. He is seventy-five
years old. And he goes to the front, inspecting, inspecting. He is
within range of enemy artillery.

L'homme libre gets a new name. Clemenceau gives his paper,
which is to say himself, the name *L'homme enchâiné*. But still, he
would rather be bound by the censor than become a minister. He
waits, he is careful, he inspires fear, and the chained man is the one
people take orders from. He calls for draconian punishments for
defeatists: prison, hard labor, death. Two Germans are picked up.
They carried a permit from Interior Minister [Louis] Malvy.
Clemenceau knows. An Austrian returns to Paris in 1915.
Clemenceau knows. There is a body of opinion in the country in
favor of a swift peace without victory, it is led by Caillaux. In

Clemenceau's opinion, Caillaux should be shot. The Right support a Clemenceau cabinet. According to General Pétain, the front-line troops support a Clemenceau cabinet.

Poincaré, his old foe, summons him to the Élysée. Clemenceau forms his cabinet in November 1917. He is ready to leap.

Clemenceau's hatred of the Germans was instinctive, gut-level, only later did it acquire a political underpinning. It is the hatred of the anarcho-conservative Gaul for the "other," the civilizing German, the machine preacher in Europe. There were only two Frenchmen who understood the German "character:" Barrès* and Clemenceau. They were the fathers of the revenge war.

The Father of the War

"'Tis war! I fear 'tis war, and I don't want the blame for it."

The kind, the good, the great Matthias Claudius† sang these lines. I can't help thinking of his poem, each time I quote Clemenceau: "*Je fais la guerre!*"

"'Tis war, I fear 'tis war!" he must have always thought and often said. But he was forced to continue: "See! I'm forced to carry part of the blame!" In answer to a question from the Socialist deputy [Pierre] Renaudel, he answered:

> I am told we should have peace. I want peace as well. But we're not going to silence Prussian militarism by grumbling! I've been asked what my policy is. Well, here it is: Domestic policy? War! Foreign policy? War! I continue to wage war! I'm trying to retain the confidence of our allies. Russia has betrayed us? I con-

*Maurice Barrès (1862–1923), French nationalist politician.
†Matthias Claudius (1740–1815), Germanic romantic poet.

tinue to wage war! Unhappy Romania is forced to capitulate? War! And I'm going to carry on until the last quarter of an hour; and then that quarter of an hour is going to belong to us!

When you listen to this old man, it's as though all the strength of the dying individualist epoch were concentrated in him before its end. The outflow of energy from the millions of soldiers and civilians, the thousands of generals, the tens of thousands of spies, agents, simple and double and triple traitors in the period is no doubt enormous, but it's not decisive. What's decisive is the last quarter of an hour, for which the old man is getting ready. He wants to feel his whole life compressed into just fifteen full and fateful minutes: prophecy, error, love, hate, revenge, patience, suffering, disappointment, defense, attack. He alone compels the Allied British and American armies to accept a unified command structure—under the overall control of the French. He, the old man, goes clambering about in trenches, in putties, with a cloak thrown over his bowed shoulders and a stick in his hand. He commands the commanders at the front, and the politicians, the civil servants, the press, the police, the manufacturers, the workers, the suppliers, the commissaries, the farmers, the workers, in the hinterland. Where does he get the strength?—It comes from patience. He can wait for the last quarter of an hour. He even teaches death to be patient. The old man will not die before the last quarter of an hour. Later, afterwards—long after that quarter of an hour has come and gone . . .

One of the last great desperate German offensives follows in July. The Battle of the Marne is decided. "Big Bertha" shells Paris. Three days later General [Charles] Mangin rolls up the left bank of the Marne. Foch is made Maréchal de France, Malvy is sentenced to five years' exile. Three more weeks—and Ludendorff concedes that a "victorious peace" is impossible. Clemenceau is seventy-seven when he dictates terms for cessation of hostilities on the Western Front. In the teeth of unwillingness on the part of the Americans, he insists on reparations. On November 8 the German negotiators come, one day before the Kaiser abdicates. At eleven, in the fifth hour of daylight, there's a cease-fire. Now it's at hand, the "last quarter of an hour."

"When the survivors march through the Arc de Triomphe," says Clemenceau in the chamber, "then we will hail them. Let them be hailed in advance for the great work of social rebuilding. Thanks to them France, which yesterday was the soldier of God, and today the soldier of humanity, will always be the soldier of the Ideal."

That's it then, the "last quarter of an hour!" Is it death's turn now? Is he not sure? Why is he not sure? Is the cup of his life not yet full? Can there be anything more than such a triumph? than complete revenge against the hated enemy? than the jubilant cries of yesterday's opponents? than the colossal sigh of the colossal peace? than the greetings of the hale survivor, and the absolving smile of the cripple? than the tears of the widows, the orphans, the bereaved fathers and mothers, who sanctified the war with the pain of their loss? Can an old man take more than the crowds outside the window roaring: "Clemenceau! Clemenceau! Clemenceau!"— the moment that, older now, older by the "last quarter of an hour" in which he has relived his whole life again, he sinks back into his armchair, exhausted? The kindly old lamp on the desk sheds its light, as ever, on the paper, empty pages, full pages. The pen waits, beside the closed inkwell. What else does he have to write? All the articles have been written, all the books, all the memoranda, all the letters. Outside the window, he hears the roar: "Clemenceau!" What else can they want from him? Hasn't he given all his speeches too? What else is there to say? There's only one thing he can call out. The old man goes up to the window, hushes the crowd, and says three words: "*Vive la France!*"

And now he's sitting there alone. Has he any friends left? Has he ever been so alone? Never, so far as he can remember; not even when—fallen, vilified, and accused of betraying France, sick, and with a bitter taste in his mouth and his heart—he sat at the editorial desk, in the smoky office; had he ever been lonely? Maybe, yes, often, almost always: He knows that. But never alone. There were colleagues there and friends, he had tasks, things to do, so many things to do! Temptations beckoned, desires distracted, dreams flattered, rage trembled, hatred shrieked, heart and brain gave birth to sentences, his pen ran, faltered, began again in fresh spate, light graying outside, lamplight still inside, a word flashed like a dagger, his tongue was as deadly as his eye; with each individual enemy hundreds fell, each one a mediocrity or a threat or a fool or a louse, and with each enemy he foiled one further hope of the great enemy: *the enemy over the border, the ancestral enemy.*

Peace arrives. Honors and laurels rain down upon him, he is elected to the Académie Française, and already he is sure he will never show his face there. Clemenceau doesn't want to give an acceptance speech. The speeches have all been spoken. And what is an honor anyway, when he already has glory? He goes to harvest it, armfuls of glory, in Metz in Lorraine, in Strasbourg in Alsace. The pictures, the photographs are well known. Strasbourg; the ecstatic populace; the girls, armfuls, throwing themselves at Poincaré and at Clemenceau.

Back into Paris, and almost from that day forth, France seems once again changed. It's no longer the country intoxicated with gratitude. Clemenceau's previous torments begin again: the daily pathetic wrangles with supplicants, ambitious mediocre enemies, people after money, after jobs.

He will be seventy-nine soon. The "last quarter of an hour" is all up; is death still hesitating? What is he waiting for? How much more can an old man stand after this last quarter of an hour? On the brink of his eighties, will he have to experience again the bitterness of his forties? Will he still have to lay down the law, watch his back, control, inspect, hate, despise—maybe even kill?

The Border

Clemenceau's political passions were ignited by Alsace-Lorraine.* Even without the lost war of 1870–71, he would probably have been an important politician, but surely not the towering statesman, French national hero, miracle of history, the stuff of international legend. Alsace-Lorraine, its loss and its reacquisition, "made" Clemenceau the hater, the avenger, the father of victory. To give a sense of the depth of his association with Alsace-Lorraine, and a sample also of the truly classical rhetoric of France, at a point where it is worthy of Demosthenes himself, we would like to include the speech that Clemenceau gave on December 8, 1918. It was the first session of the French chamber after victory. The speech is addressed to the first delegation of deputies from Alsace-Lorraine to sit in a French parliament for almost half a century:

> Brothers from Alsace-Lorraine! Victorious France clasps you to its heart. Out of a terrible drama of tears and blood now flows an infinitely rejoicing sweetness.
>
> During the bitterest crisis of this terrible tragedy, I was there, in Bordeaux, when I saw you torn from our arms; in chains you

*The provinces of Alsace-Lorraine, ceded to Germany after the French defeat in the Franco-Prussian War (1870–71), were restored to France by the Treaty of Versailles. (From 1940 to 1944 they were again under German rule.)

walked at the triumph of barbarism. Kuss, your standard bearer, the mayor of Strasbourg, falls like an oak struck by lightning. And the National Assembly, as proud as we are today, shaken by a fatal convulsion, looked on as you filed by, upright, silent, frozen in unhappiness, but—as were we all—full of hope and resolve.

That was because we were all France, we could not stop being France, together or sundered—we were France, because you took a piece of France away with you, and kept a piece of France with you, safe from defilement by the enemy. That piece of France you now bring back with you from those days of oppression, which, thanks to you, were days of pride.

By chance, it is the last survivor of the number who protested on that day who today rises, in accord with the representatives of the nation, in the name of the government, and in the midst of the patriotic enthusiasm of the republic, to call out to you a blazing word of welcome; a word that officially seals your beautiful and moving return to us for all perpetuity.

There are emotions that human language may not express. That we understand one another, that we love one another, that we may more intimately be connected one with another in the blissful hours of national experience—a look, or a gesture, is sufficient! They already reveal the devotion in our souls.

But the future will not wait, and the reconquered state will be the arena for new tasks, an imposing list of new duties. May the thought of this day remain present in us, to be more beautiful the more we draw on it for courage to act in the future. Is it not a question of deflecting the constant threat of painful fatalities from our chosen path? Those circumstances attend all peoples who are drawn to great tasks. We accept the challenge of the inevitable! Let us, beginning with this resplendent day of the union of all Frenchmen, never cease to let France rise higher in the eyes of all men, and in the love of its children.

In the hard school of this most decisive test, we have already learned the need to be unified, to defend the most vital interests of the fatherland. Men of Alsace and Lorraine! You, whose presence in our midst occasions so much joy after so much sorrow—you be the witnesses, the guarantors that, aside from all healthy and natural differences of opinion, a constant defense of France may not be had without a never-ending strengthening of the natural friendship among all French people.

Our celebration today marks no ephemeral change! It is necessary that our experiences survive the daily clash of opinion that is the necessary mark of a democratic regime. But if one day we should forget ourselves, then may one of you rise, to remind us with a word, with a sign, of our higher duties.

Lest we misunderstand: We must develop a force, create an energetic order, of the kind that history has thus far only ever demonstrated in violent enterprises. This is the problem of our age: on the one hand, the endeavor to maintain; on the other, the inclination to renew—to move from the policy of conquest, to the organisation of peacetime. . . .

For Clemenceau, Alsace-Lorraine, whose return he hailed with such warmth and ceremony, was more than just another French province. In Alsace, in Lorraine, French patriotism posted its vanguard. A vanguard is "covered"; it is never "protected." Related, but not tied to Germany (or German-ness) by its Alemannic dialect, a mixed and forever evolving population leaving it apparently often uncertain of its loyalties, these border provinces are as incomprehensible to the Frenchman of the South or the interior, as they are on the German side to the Brandenburger, the Thuringian, or the Bavarian. The blinkered thinking of those people who for the last century or so have been writing our history has, since the truly macabre invention of "distinct nation-states," loved tidy borders, and is incapable of understanding gradations, nuances, and shadings. But Alsace-Lorraine is one of the "nuances." For the historian it's a source of complications; for the politician, a nagging reproach. As soon as mediocre politicians are reminded of Alsace-Lorraine, they think European reality is accusing them of lacking imagination. They view Alsace-Lorraine as an "international" problem; in fact it is a French one. The German-inflected French that the Alsatian speaks is evidence that national boundaries do *not* have to be language boundaries; for the sake of simplicity—almost, one is tempted to say, for the sake of banality—nationality problems in Europe are very often confounded with language problems. It's such an easy matter, if one's ethnopsychology is insufficient, to call in philology for advice!

Alsace is where the French Revolution encounters French patriotism. Clemenceau's Jacobinism meets Barrès's Chauvinism. A French revolutionary, even if he belongs to an international party, finds his national home and his revolutionary feeling both expressed in one song: the "Marseillaise." It is no accident that the home of the "Marseillaise" lies in the dangerous fringe territories of France. It is no accident that the "Internationale" has become a popular and party-meeting hymn in France, nothing more. Nor is it an accident that the "Marseillaise," composed on the banks of the Rhine, should bear its southern harbor name. It is the whole of France, from the Rhine to the Mediterranean. It is France from Jacobinism to patriotism. It is France from revolutionary to conservative.[. . .]

Peace and Retirement

On December 30 [1918], Clemenceau addresses a war-weary and peace-hopeful assembly. There's a childish festive mood: the happy credulous representatives of the people are giving themselves to the happy dream of a world gone good. An understandable reaction to such a mighty outburst of human bestiality. A banal saying, echoing in uncritical ears from childhood primers, says it's best to be magnanimous in victory. The pious dream of the American,* who has such an infantile interpretation of the Bible's scenes and prophecies that he thinks man can achieve the dream of the prophet pretty much on the spot, at the first opportunity, and omitting the Last Judgment, bring about the time "when the lion pastures with the lamb . . . and their young play together"† gave us the League of Nations in the usual double-quick time. The vanquished lion was not invited to the pastures where the lambs were grazing in Geneva. But it was planned to invite him along a little later, once he had given proof that he had at least stopped roaring. So he was quiet. As we know.

Clemenceau had a better understanding of carnivores. On that December 30, Père Victoire and le Tigre** in one, he said that he preferred the old politics of a balance of powers in Europe to any League of Nations, and best of all were well secured borders. In January, a delegation of French representatives takes part in the peace conference. The most important delegate after Clemenceau himself was, without doubt, [André] Tardieu, a gifted journalist, politician, and negotiator. Clemenceau chaired the conference. In February an attempt was made on his life. He was wounded. It wasn't a serious wound, but the attempt provoked a stir in cabinets, parliaments, editorial offices, and stock exchanges. The wound began to heal after a day or two. The old tiger got ready to perform some more leaps. The devout Wilson tried to rein him in. "The only man since Jesus Christ," thus

*A reference to U.S. President Woodrow Wilson (1856–1924).

†A paraphrase of Isaiah 11:6.

**Two of Clemenceau's popular nicknames.

Clemenceau of Wilson, "who thinks he's a peacemaker. He thinks he's the second Messiah." Clemenceau even went so far as to call in the bill for past assistance: He reminded the president that Lafayette and Rochambeau hadn't fought in the American War of Independence out of cold calculation. The Messiah doesn't want to give up his scheme. He wants the Germans to keep the Saar and the coal mines there. Finally they reach a compromise, as we know: France gets the use of the coal mines, and the population of the Saar is offered a plebiscite. It's not Clemenceau's last battle with the Anglo-Saxons. Things even get physical between the old man and Lloyd George. Clemenceau offers satisfaction, pistols or sabers.

An agreement was reached. The Germans signed on June 28.* But the foreign policy success was to cost Clemenceau dearly. In Paris a general strike has broken out. The Russian revolution has obviously provoked something of an echo. As other forms of public protest are prohibited, the strikers send a deputation of war widows to the War Ministry. Clemenceau has them broken up by the police. The courts acquit the murderer of Jaures. On May 1, Paris is left without power, water, or public transportation. The workers attack the police. Shots are fired. A column of demonstrators send some war wounded up ahead, cripples on sticks, blind, the "*gueules cassées.*" The police doesn't scruple to shoot at them. The general strike lasts into June. Not until the day of the victory celebrations does unity return to the country.

The elections in November seem likely to bring down Clemenceau's government. Will Clemenceau run for president of the Republic? He is too proud to offer his candidacy. He himself dashed the hopes of the Catholics that as president, he would

*The Treaty of Versailles was signed on June 28, 1919.

reopen channels with the Vatican. When his friends worked toward a candidacy, he disowned them. [Paul] Deschanel became prime minister. Clemenceau did not receive him personally. He had him not so much welcomed as snubbed by his cabinet secretary. Clemenceau's cabinet stood down.[. . .]

January 17, 1920

50

From an Author's Diary

Monday,
in the fourth year of the German apocalypse

This morning author's copies arrived of my new book—two large, brown-paper parcels, well-secured with string to give to friends. I won't open the parcels. Most of my friends are writers themselves. I hope they confine themselves to reading the works of the immortal dead. New books—especially those bearing dedications—seem to take up more room than bought or borrowed sets of the classics. Some of my friends have apartments, wives, children, libraries. They reserve a special shelf for books by their friends. Maybe they would put my book there too. But a little reluctantly, I think. You can't easily get rid of books with personal dedications. "To my old friend!", "Cordially!", "Salutations!" Most of these phrases remind me of the old proverb, not always true, that "one crow won't peck another in the eye." So I won't open my parcels, and I won't write any dedications. It's my eighteenth book. Of the previous seventeen, fifteen have been forgotten. In Germany the forgotten ones have also been banned. Outside Germany you're hardly likely to come across one in a bookshop. The odd cultured fool—poor men, as a rule—sometimes comes up and tells me he's read one or other of my forgotten books.

Thursday

Today the publisher's royalty statement on my seventeenth book arrived. A total of 3,450 copies have been sold. I am a long way from having "earned back" my advance. Under the accounts it says: "Errors possible" and "Any objections must be received within two weeks." To what am I to object? If anything, to the phrase, "Errors possible." If there are any errors, then they certainly won't have been in my favor. My publisher is an honorable man. In his accompanying letter, he writes, and I quote: "It's terrible to see these accounts. The advances are not covered." I have had seven publishers already. He is the eighth. That means I have had dealings with eight honorable men. That's a lot—in a writer's life as short as mine has been. And I'm not their only author. My colleagues' advances are not covered either. Book publishing is a weird and wonderful business. Publishers deal in red figures. It must be very hard, especially when you bear in mind that I can't live off my advances either.

Friday

What I said about publishers yesterday was unfair. I assume they are really an equivalent of patrons. Maybe they love literature more than I do, and yet they don't follow that "inner voice" that we writers appeal to. Maybe they should, the publishers, because they make no profits on what they publish, they make losses—as I see from my statements. The poor fools! They publish German books at a time when German has less currency than Esperanto or Latin. German, I mean to say, as it is—still—written by a handful of us. There is another variety, written and spoken by others, and that, admittedly, is very widely used. This schism in the German language must be a confusing thing for the rest of the world. The British and French must think what Hitler speaks is German, not least because Hitler's victims rarely understand German. But the national catastrophe has been visible for a long time in the ravaged state of the language. That the German reader doesn't understand writers of good German, like you and like me—we'd gotten accustomed to that. But now we can't depend on foreigners either. An Englishman, a Frenchman, an Italian, once he's spent an hour in the company of a Hitler, a Ribbentrop, or a Goebbels, will never again be able to understand our language. It will be Chinese to him, just as the German spoken in the Third Reich is to us. Hitler's German is about as good as Stalin's Russian. The last dictator who had any proficiency in his mother tongue was Julius Ceasar. We have no information about Alexander the Great. Frederick II could speak neither French nor German. Napoleon spoke French like an "immigrant," even though he could recite Corneille (or was it Racine?) by heart. But then his regime was based on the winning of battles rather than on literary publications. "Deeds, not words," as the "Führer" used to say. Mussolini is a good editorial writer from the old *Avanti* school, but as a writer he's no better than an Italian Friedrich Stampfer. A speech isn't a write. Dictators all speak too much.

Sunday

It's a masochistic pleasure to read newspapers, not every day but once a week, on Sunday, at the height of the weekend, which is one of the most important factors in politics since the beginning of the apocalypse. Whatever good and useful thoughts and decisions begin to burgeon in democratic statesmen on Friday afternoons have begun to evaporate by Saturday afternoon. But tyrants don't have weekends. God created the world in six days, and on the seventh He rested. Peaceful statesmen rest on the sixth *and* seventh. For forty-eight hours they celebrate the Lord's day. They exceed the demands of religion, and they overdo the example set by the Almighty. It's a striking thing that *dictators don't play golf.* Their Sabbath is not reserved for sport, but for surprises. Golf bears a considerable responsibility for the end of the civilized world. Napoleon played chess, Prince Eugene played dominoes. Politicians have fewer good ideas on the greens than they once did on the much-reviled "green baize." On Christmas 1916, I was at the front. Our divisional staff, the colonel, the company commander, were all getting ready for a well-deserved "breather." They had forgotten that our opponents, the Russians, celebrated Christmas two weeks later than we did.* They took advantage of our peaceful celebrations and launched a surprise attack on us, distracted as we were by Christmas lights and pious thoughts. Two weeks later we duly retaliated, but without success, because they were waiting for us. It's a pity the democratic statesmen didn't serve at the front, especially the Eastern Front. Dictators always postpone Christmas by a couple of weeks. Democrats are always sticklers for punctual Christmases and punctual Sundays, thanks to which they have been able to celebrate many glorious victories: on the golf course.

Wednesday

I am told "in confidence," but I have no compunction in making it public, that a mediocre German writer who emigrated—I don't know why—has declined to work on a newly founded periodical

---

*Because of the difference between the Julian and Gregorian calendars, not adopted by Russia until 1918.

because Jews also worked on it. Here, then, is the case of an émigré who still lives by the Nuremberg laws. He's living in Zurich; why didn't he stay in Nuremberg? There are several émigrés who didn't flee on account of their "Jewish grandmothers," but because of their "Aryan" grandmothers, and who claim a position of honor within the émigré community by virtue of not being Jews. They live among Christians and Jews, with their Aryan grandmothers. And they are fairly successful, because a lot of émigrés with Jewish grandmothers take the emigration of an anti-Semite for a heroic act, and are moved to tears at the sight of blond mice. Certainly it's "bad luck" to be Jewish. But it's precisely that that makes it vulgar, especially outside the Third Reich, to claim laurels that should have fallen to their poor grandmother. Ever since the end of illiteracy, so many janitors are writing German! . . . The émigré janitors are published by Jewish publishing houses. A German anti-Semite who stays home is an honorable man. But the other, who emigrates and publishes his books in the company of Jews, is a plebeian. He ought to be living off confiscated assets, not royalties.

Thursday

Curious that in spite of all sorts of personal adversity, one should still be so preoccupied by what the "others" are doing, and by the "political situation" as a whole. I am presented with the—very modest—reckoning of the hotel where I enjoy more credit than comfort. I set the hotel bill next to the publisher's accounts. The comparison prompts me to publish an extract from my diary. I am no longer up to thinking of "a subject" for "an article." I tear a couple of pages out of my diary and send them off, like a message in a bottle.

Das Neue Tagebuch (Paris), September 4, 1937

Index

Joseph Roth was born Moses Joseph Roth to Jewish parents on September 2, 1894, in Brody in Galicia, in the extreme east of the then Habsburg Empire; he died on May 27, 1939, in Paris. He never saw his father—who disappeared before he was born and later died insane—but grew up with his mother and her relatives. After completing school in Brody, he matriculated at the University of Lemberg (variously Lvov or Lviv), before transferring to the University of Vienna in 1914. He served for a year or two with the Austro-Hungarian Army on the Eastern Front—though possibly only as an army journalist or censor. Later he was to write: "My strongest experience was the War and the destruction of my fatherland, the only one I ever had, the Dual Monarchy of Austria-Hungary."

In 1918 he returned to Vienna, where he began writing for left-wing papers, occasionally as "Red Roth," "*der rote Roth*." In 1920 he moved to Berlin, and in 1923 he began his distinguished association with the *Frankfurter Zeitung*. In the following years he traveled throughout Europe, filing copy for the *Frankfurter* from the south of France, the USSR, Albania, Germany, Poland, and Italy. He was one of the most distinguished and best-paid journalists of the period—being paid at the dream rate of one deutsche mark per line. Some of his pieces were collected under the title of one of them, *The Panopticum on Sunday* (1928), while some of his reportage from the Soviet Union went into *The Wandering Jews*. His gifts of style and perception could, on occasion, overwhelm his subjects, but he was a journalist of singular compassion. He observed and warned of the rising Nazi scene in Germany (Hitler actually appears by name in Roth's first novel, in 1923), and his 1926 visit to the USSR disabused him of most—but not quite all—of his sympathy for Communism.

When the Nazis took power in Germany in 1933, Roth immediately severed all his ties with the country. He lived in Paris—where he had been based for some years—but also in Amsterdam, Ostend, and the south of

France, and wrote for émigré publications. His royalist politics were mainly a mask for his pessimism; his last article was called "Goethe's Oak at Buchenwald." His final years were difficult; he moved from hotel to hotel, drinking heavily, worried about money and the future. What precipitated his final collapse was hearing the news that the playwright Ernst Toller had hanged himself in New York. An invitation from the American PEN Club (the organization that had brought Thomas Mann and many others to the States) was found among Roth's papers. It is tantalizing but ultimately impossible to imagine him taking ship to the New World, and continuing to live and to write: His world was the old one, and he'd used it all up.

Roth's fiction came into being alongside his journalism, and in the same way: at café tables, at odd hours and all hours, peripatetically, chaotically, charmedly. His first novel, *The Spider's Web*, was published in installments in 1923. There followed *Hotel Savoy* and *Rebellion* (both 1924), hard-hitting books about contemporary society and politics; then *Flight Without End*, *Zipper and His Father*, and *Right and Left* (all *Heimkehrerromane*—novels about soldiers returning home after war). *Job* (1930) was his first book to draw considerably on his Jewish past in the East. *The Radetzky March* (1932) has the biggest scope of all his books and is commonly reckoned his masterpiece. There follows the books he wrote in exile, books with a stronger fabulist streak in them, full of melancholy beauty: *Tarabas, The Hundred Days, Confession of a Murderer, Weights and Measures, The Emperor's Tomb*, and *The Tale of the 1002nd Night*.

Michael Hofmann, the son of the German novelist Gert Hofmann, was born in 1957 in Freiburg. At the age of four, he moved to England, where he has lived off and on ever since. After studying English at Cambridge and comparative literature on his own, he moved to London in 1983. He has published poems and reviews widely in England and in the United States. In 1993, he was appointed Distinguished Lecturer in the English Department of the University of Florida at Gainesville.

To date, he has published four books of poems and a collection of criticism, *Behind the Lines*, all with Faber & Faber. He edited (with James Lasdun) a book of contemporary versions of the *Metamorphoses*, called *After Ovid*, and is editing *Rilke in English* for Penguin.

Hofmann has translated works by Bertolt Brecht, Franz Kafka, Wolfgang Koeppen, and Gert Hoffman, among others, and is the translator of the last eight Joseph Roth titles to appear in English, including *The Tale of the 1002nd Night*, for which he was awarded the PEN/Book-of-the-Month Club Prize for Translation in 1998; *Rebellion*, for which he was awarded the Helen and Kurt Wolff Translation Prize in 2000; and *The Radetzky March*, in an edition so far only available from Granta in the United Kingdom (2002). He is currently working on a biographical selection of Roth's letters.